MALCOLM X AND AFRICA

MALCOLM X AND AFRICA

A.B. Assensoh and Yvette M. Alex-Assensoh

Cambria African Studies Series
General Editor: Toyin Falola
Associate Editor: Moses Ochonu

CAMBRIA
PRESS

Amherst, New York

This book is dedicated to some important persons in our lives: Mrs. Thelma Coleman Alex of Breaux Bridge, Louisiana, USA, and her grandchildren, who are our own children: Kwadwo Stephen Alex Assensoh, Livingston Alex Kwabena Assensohn, and Livia Yvette Alex; as well as three remarkable deceased scholarly colleagues: Professor Ali A. Mazrui of Kenya (Mwalimu and Nana of Ghana royalty honor) who was, Columbia University alumnus as well as a graduate of Manchester and Oxford Universities; Professor Lawrence J. Hanks (Brother Larry, as we affably called him), a Morehouse College graduate and a Government (Politics) doctorate (Ph.D.) from Harvard University. Finally but not the least, we also remember our Pan-African Brother, Dr. Tajudeen Abdul-Raheem, a Rhodes Scholar and an Oxford University doctoral degree (D. Phil) recipient. May they rest in perfect peace until we meet again!

Table of Contents

FOREWORD

MALCOLM X: A TRUE FRIEND OF AFRICA

I was very young in the mid–1960s when Malcolm X began visiting African countries. Indeed, I was innocent of the world around me; in particular, I was unlearned about the plight of African Americans as reflected in the writings and speeches of Malcolm X. I lived in Igboland, which formed part of the then Eastern Region of Nigeria, where the great author of *Things Fall Apart* (Professor Chinua Achebe) also came from. Nigeria's four regions were later to be carved into states at the onset of the 1967–1970 Nigerian civil war, an exercise that was repeated over and over in the quest of officialdom to bring government closer to the people.

Also, in the early 1960s, Nigeria had a parliamentary system of government headed by a prime minister, who at the time was Alhaji Sir Abubakar Tafawa Balewa of the Northern People's Congress (NPC) political party. Dr. Nnamdi Azikiwe of the National Council of Nigerian Citizens (NCNC) was the nominal head of state, first as the first indigenous governor-general, and then as president, when the country became a republic. Both of these positions were ceremonial as the prime minister— similar to the case in the United Kingdom—has executive powers as the elected head of government.

When Malcolm X arrived in Nigeria on May 6, 1964, from Cairo, Egypt, the capital of our country was Lagos; today the country's administrative capital is called Abuja, while the city of Lagos remains the country's commercial capital. I was barely four years old at the time, with Nigeria having attained her independence from the United Kingdom in 1960. Malcolm X arrived in the West African nation of over 170 million people as part of a planned visit to the Western African subregion and other regions of Africa as a true friend of the continent. The late Columbia University professor Manning Marable in *A Life of Reinvention: Malcolm X* (2011) gave it the best description when he described the type of place Nigeria was upon the arrival of the black Muslim leader (Malcolm X). Marable wrote that unlike the North African nation of Egypt from where Malcolm X had departed for Nigeria, it was a different emotional feeling for Malcolm because, upon arrival, he saw nothing but black faces. That made it dawn on him that "he had landed in the center of the long historical struggle that had increasingly found expression in his rhetoric back in Harlem" (Marable 2011, 313). In a way, Malcolm X was happy that he was visiting a true African country, where fellow blacks controlled not only the political positions, but the destiny of the nation.

In fact, my parents were enlightened enough to remember that barely four years after our country's independence, a tall and handsome black American came from New York to visit the then Western Region of Nigeria, and that his name, as the newspapers reported, was Malcolm X. We heard that he was born in America, and that he was named Malcolm Little at birth, but he later changed his name to Malcolm X to protest at having been given what he considered to be a slave name. At the time in 1964, Nigeria was at peace, and the country was relatively prosperous in economic and political fortunes. However, Professor Marable, like several other Western critics, still deemed it necessary to put it bluntly that when Malcolm X arrived in Nigeria, he found a nation that was trying to cope with the effects of fierce internecine political battles. In fact, two years after Malcolm's historic visit to Nigeria, the country "would descend into a nightmare of military dictatorship from which it would not emerge for decades" (Marable 2011, 313).

That nightmare was a fierce bloodbath necessitated by a civil war that erupted following the attempt of our Eastern Region to secede from the Nigerian Federation and the to rename the region as the Republic of Biafra (the reasons for the secession are not discussed here as my foreword is about Malcolm X). Irrespective of Nigeria's subsequent difficulties, Malcolm X would have still considered the country—just as he felt about the other African nations he visited in Western and Eastern Africa—as a viable part of what African Americans like himself (such as the late Rev. Dr. Martin Luther King, Jr., Rev. Jesse Jackson, Sr., and others) called the motherland.

In preparing to write this foreword to this very important book about a crucial aspect of Malcolm X's life, I found that his visit to Nigeria in May 1964 was not his last. He left the Kenyan capital of Nairobi and travelled to Nigeria again on October 28, 1964. He also made a brief visit to the Ethiopian capital of Addis Ababa. On hand to welcome Malcolm X during his second visit to Nigeria was his very good friend, University of Ibadan professor E. Essien-Udom, whom he had known for many years in the United States. In his published autobiography, Malcolm confirmed that he and the Ibadan don were extremely happy to be in each other's company. Malcolm X had noted in the autobiography that he and Dr. Essien-Udom had known each other in America when this prolific political scientist, in Malcolm's words, "researched the Nation of Islam for his book, *Black Nationalism*" (Malcolm X 1999, 356).

The available records have indicated that, during Malcolm X's second visit to Nigeria, he had the opportunity to address large gatherings, which included students, whom he considered to be future leaders of the country. One such gathering was at Trenchard Hall of the University of Ibadan at which he appealed to the students as well as leaders of freed African nations throughout the continent to support their fellow blacks (once called Negroes but known as African Americans) and, if possible, to redress before the United Nations on their behalf what he considered to be their sad political plight in the United States, including their continued suffering of racism. It is in this book, for the first time, that I have read about some of the reasons why Malcolm X did not get the support that he sought in Nigeria, especially for his political agenda in the interests of himself and other blacks back home. Yet, Malcolm X felt a lot of acceptance in his interaction with the people, especially as he felt deeply honored and touched when an ethnic Yoruba name of "Omowale" was bestowed on him. He learned from his Nigerian friends that the new name meant "the son who has come home" (Malcolm X 1999, 357).

Apart from radio and television appearances, Malcolm had the opportunity to pay visits to several important Nigerian political leaders, including Dr. Nnamdi Azikiwe, who impressed the African American Muslim leader. He saw Dr. Azikiwe as a leader with a profound knowledge of events in the United States, including "a good grasp of the key players in the U.S. civil rights struggle" (Marable 2011, 374; Assensoh and Alex-Assensoh 2014; 81).

One learns a great deal about Malcolm X's foray into several parts of Africa in 1964 from his published memoirs, which he completed with the assistance of Alex Haley, the world-renowned author of *Roots*—the book and TV series that detailed the story of his own Gambian ancestral roots. As I read about the book in later years, it sold over six million copies in hardcover and won for Haley a Pulitzer Prize and a National Book Award. It is well known that although Malcolm X was very busy, he still found the time to dictate the story of his life to Haley. Haley purportedly edited the story mildly and, after Malcolm X's unfortunate assassination in 1965 at the age of thirty-nine (just like Dr. King later), had the manuscript published posthumously. Alex Haley died in February 1992 at the age of seventy.

Since Malcolm X was assassinated in 1965, I never had the chance to meet him in person. However, I am happy to point out the fact that through superbly written publications like this work by Professors Assensoh and

Alex-Assensoh (including Malcolm X's autobiography), I feel today that I am very well acquainted with this great and heroic leader. His leadership role, as a Muslim and a civil rights activist, prompted the United States Postal Service, on January 20, 1999, to issue a special commemorative postal stamp to honor him. In the words of his oldest daughter (Attallah), that act of recognition on the part of American officialdom "affirms the integrity of his [Malcolm X's] heart and the wisdom of his philosophy, and guarantees that his message will endure" (Malcolm X 1999, x).

It is also very important for me to point out the fact that irrespective of my own busy professional life, I still took the time to peruse the manuscript for this book, coauthored by professors A.B. Assensoh and Yvette M. Alex-Assensoh, my wonderful intellectual friends and colleagues, who are currently based at University of Oregon. To say the least, I am very impressed with the contents. In fact, I knew that the intellectual couple was doing research to have articles and a book published about Malcolm X when I visited their home in Bloomington, Indiana as a guest and also as one of the active participants in Indiana University's celebration of the professor emeritus elevation of "A.B." (as he is affably called by all of us as his friends). That was in 2011 during which time several of us in the visiting celebratory group took part in the panel discussion at Indiana University from which grew the scholarly contributions that formed part of the book published in 2014 to honor Professor Assensoh's achievements.

Titled *Intellectual Agent, Mediator and Interlocutor: A.B. Assensoh and African Politics in Transition*, the 350-page book contains my co-authored chapter, which shows my high regard for the Assensohs. Therefore, I found it very easy to accept the invitation to write the foreword to this book, which will benefit many people from all walks of life, both scholars and readers of the general public, who do not know the extent of Malcolm X's relationship with Africa, including the two visits he paid to the continent, the most extensive of which was in 1964, as I have endeavored to describe above. In 2014, the Assensohs completed a short biography of Malcolm X, which is very suitable for classroom use, and I am very impressed that they decided to produce a separate book that deals with several aspects of Malcolm X's relationship with Africa and several African leaders, including diplomats. It is, indeed, a publication that provides a lot of useful information about Malcolm X and Africa.

For example, I did not know beforehand that Malcolm X visited and stayed on in Africa for so many months in 1964. Another revelation that has fascinated my family and me from this publication is that if Malcolm X had not been assassinated in 1965, he was planning to move his entire family to live in an African country. Therefore, it is my sincere hope that other readers will enjoy perusing the book and, just as I did, discover several important details about the life and times of Malcolm X and his family, who have remained faithful to the cause that he led and for which he was martyred in the Audubon Ballroom, when an assassin's bullet in 1965 unsuccessfully attempted to silence him forever. The assassin and his accomplices tried their best, but his children, named after several great African heroes, have lived to carry on the torch that their father lit. Attallah Shabazz, indeed, is the oldest daughter; the others are Gamilah Lumumba Shabazz, named for Egypt's late president Gamal Abdel Nasser and the Democratic Republic of Congo (DRC) late prime minister Patrice Lumumba; the others were Ilyasah Shabazz; Quibilah Shabazz; Malika Shabazz; and Malika Shabazz.

Before ending this foreword, I want to take the opportunity to pay a special tribute to his late widow (Betty) as well as the Malcolm X children, all of whom happened to be daughters. Like the children of the late Rev. Dr. Martin Luther King, Jr. and other martyred black leaders, they have continued to propagate the very message their fathers promoted and for which they died, often at the hands of assassins. They should also consider Africa—as their parents did—the motherland, which is yearning for them to either visit or to move and stay, if they wish.

As they might have learned already, their parents were often very much at home when they visited the African continent; Dr. King, for example, did so with his wife (Coretta) when both of them were invited to visit Ghana in 1957 by the late president Kwame Nkrumah to participate in the March 6th independence celebrations, during which time the Gold Coast had her name changed to Ghana. Malcolm and other brave black leaders from the American diaspora, including Muhammad Ali (the former Cassius Clay), also followed the footsteps of Dr. King as well as Dr. W.E.B. DuBois to visit the motherland. The remains of the indomitable Dr. DuBois, along with George Padmore, regarded as the father of Pan-Africanism, have been interred in Ghana, whose flag still beams with Marcus Garvey's black star in the middle!

Damien Ejigiri, PhD,
Dean, Graduate School, Southern University,
Baton Rouge, Louisiana, USA

PREFACE

WHAT AFRICA MEANT FOR MALCOLM X

The 'Malcolm X Committee' rushed me from the Chinese Embassy dinner to where a soiree in my honor had already begun at the Press Club. It was my first sight of Ghanaians dancing the high life...I was pressed to make a short speech. I stressed again the need for unity between Africans and Afro-Americans. I cried out of my heart: 'Now, dance! Sing! But as you do—remember [Nelson] Mandela, remember Sobokwe [Robert M. Sobukwe]! Remember [Patrice] Lumumba in his grave! Remember South Africans now in jail!'

—Malcolm X, with Alex Haley, 1999

Malcolm X, whose words are quoted above, had a big heart for Africa. He also had a big vision for what he saw as African-*cum*-African American relationship; as pointed out elsewhere, he always had unity at the core of his perception of the relationship among the continent that he visited, its people, and Malcolm's fellow blacks in the United States. Therefore, if he had lived beyond February 1965, when he was done to death by an assassin's bullet, he could have utilized—for the benefit of Pan-Africanism as well as the nurturing of black unity in general—part of the vast experiences that he gained from Africa between April 1964 and November

1964, when he lived on the continent in a special pilgrimage, whereby he was forced by circumstances to stay away from his pregnant wife (Betty), who was expecting their twin daughters, an achievement that makes both the father and mother the envy of many; among the Akan people of Ghana, Malcolm or his wife (Betty) would be described by the Akan word *Owonta* (or creator of twins). As confirmed by Columbia University's late professor Manning Marable, the long period that Malcolm X stayed away from his pregnant wife constituted "the twenty-four weeks from April through November 1964, when Malcolm was out of the United States [visiting Africa]" (Marable 2011, 374).

As quoted in the introduction, Malcolm X was speaking at a Ghana Press Club event in Accra, the country's capital, during one of his two consecutive journeys to the West African subregion, and indeed to Ghana, where he had come to amass many friends among the indigenous population and also from the friendly ranks of those that the University of Michigan professor Kevin K. Gaines described in his 2006 book as "American Africans" in Ghana.

Malcolm X was a black leader imbued with tenets of Pan-Africanism and he was also very much conscious of African history. He invoked the names of Nelson Mandela (1918–2013) and Robert M. Sobukwe (1924–1978), both of whom were stalwarts of the anti-apartheid nationalist struggle in South Africa, and who were at the time spending years in apartheid jails. Malcolm X admired both men and, from his extensive readings, had come to know about their political circumstances very well. Sobukwe, born in December 1924, was one of the founders of the African Nationalist Congress (ANC) while Mr. Mandela, born in July 1918, was considered—in African terminology—a senior to Sobukwe because he was about six years older than Sobukwe. By his own birth circumstances, Malcolm X (born in 1925) was one year younger than Sobukwe but about seven years the junior of Mandela; therefore, in African parlance, Malcolm was bound to show reverence for both men, irrespective of either of their accomplishments or status in the anti-apartheid struggle.

According to South African black politics, of which Malcolm X was also very much familiar, Sobukwe eventually became dissatisfied with ANC politics, just as Malcolm was himself later in life unhappy with the black Islamic group, the Nation of Islam (NOI). As a result, Sobukwe left to form the Pan-African National Congress (PANC), of which he was president in 1959, while Malcolm X too left the NOI to form two radical groups to propagate his principles and leadership ideas. Furthermore, in a rare move, after Sobukwe's studies at Fort Hare, where he joined the African Nationalist Youth Council (ANYC), Sobukwe in 1954 moved to Johannesburg, where he became a lecturer of African Studies at the University of the Witwatersrand (Wits). Before that, in 1950, he had been appointed as a teacher at a high school in Standerton, a position Sobukwe lost when he spoke out in favor of the black defiance campaign in 1952, but which was later reinstated. During this period, the young Sobukwe was not directly involved with mainstream ANC activities, but still held the position of secretary of the organization's branch in Standerton.

It is very impressive that as far back as in the 1960s, Malcolm X would invoke the names of Mandela and Sobukwe at an event in Ghana. That act, to a large extent, showed how dedicated Malcolm X was to Africa and the study of its historical figures. He also invoked the name of Patrice Lumumba, the first prime minister of the Congo, whose name was changed to Zaire and is today the Democratic Republic of the Congo (DRC). In fact, Malcolm X was such a great admirer of Lumumba that he named one of his daughters after him. It is also reassuring that in his published autobiography, he remembered these Pan-Africanist leaders as well as those imprisoned at the time for their nationalist activities. Malcolm X, indeed, showed that he was thoughtful as well as endowed with a strong memory because he did not want his Ghanaian audience to enjoy themselves, including dabbling heavily in high-life dancing and merrymaking and forget all about Mandela, Sobukwe, Lumumba, and others, who had suffered for their anti-colonialist activities.

For example, Malcolm X did not only remember prime minister Patrice Lumumba as a Congolese leader, who was in fact born the same year of his own birth (1925), but he also did indeed remember him as an African leader who was assassinated on February 11, 1961, about four years before the unfortunate assassination of Malcolm X himself. He, therefore, told his Ghanaian audience to remember him in his grave, which would obviously be very touching for those who heard Malcolm utter those words.

Malcolm X's Ghanaian audience might have been surprised that an African American, who was not one of them as an indigenous African, would know very much about Lumumba, a very beloved and close friend of their own late president Kwame Nkrumah, whose book *The Challenge of the Congo* detailed some of the sad events that led to the untimely death of the charismatic Congolese nationalist leader of the then Belgian Congo. However, Malcolm, as a Harlem resident in the United States, was very much aware of the fact that, as Professor Marable reported in his biography of Malcolm X, Premier Lumumba, upon his odyssey and subsequent death, had "come to be recognized as a symbol for postcolonial African aspirations" (Marable 2011, 189).

In fact, Malcolm X and other diaspora-based black leaders, especially those of the United States, who were in the thick of the Congolese events, were very much aware of the fact that it was on January 17, 1961, that Lumumba was assassinated in the Katanga Province of the then Congo, and that the announcement of his death at the United Nations in February 1961 led to anti-UN demonstrations, in which Malcolm X was heavily involved. The demonstrations, which also took place in several African countries, stemmed from the fact that Pan-Africanists, like Malcolm X, Ghana's late president Kwame Nkrumah, and others, felt that the UN had failed to adequately protect the lawfully elected Congolese leader (Lumumba). Additionally, there were also widespread but unsuccessful calls for Swedish-born United Nations' secretary-general

Dag Hammarskjold to step down from his prestigious international position.

Also, when there were riots as part of the aftermath of the announcement of the death of Lumumba, United Nations officials, like U.S. ambassador Adlai Stevenson, and New York City officials blamed the widespread local disturbances on Malcolm X and other radical Islamic elements. Instead of making Malcolm X feel or look bad, the events seemed to have added to the popularity of the young, national Muslim leader. To show his increased stature or prestige, it was reported that the writer, the late Maya Angelou, and a friend contacted the NOI to arrange a meeting with Malcolm X, which took place at a restaurant owned by the NOI in uptown New York area. After that, Malcolm X, who had been sobered by the assassination of Lumumba, an African leader that he respected very much, decided to devote a lot of his time to his pastoral duties in Mosque No. 7, where he lectured on a variety of topics. However, part of his lectures was couched in the following quoted words: "In the next war, the War of Armageddon, it will be a race war and will not be a 'spooky war'" (Marable 2011, 190).

With everything considered, it was not very surprising, at the time, that Malcolm X and Betty named one of their six daughters Gamilah Lumumba Shabazz in honor of the slain Congolese prime minister. It is shown that her first name, Gamilah, was also in honor of Egyptian president Gamal Abdul Nasser, a staunch pro-African unity leader, whose country hosted the 1964 annual meeting of the African heads of state meeting of the Organization of African Unity (OAU) in Cairo, which was attended by Malcolm X as an organizational black leader from the diaspora, indeed as the founder of the Organization of Afro-American Unity (OAAU) and Muslim Mosque, Inc.

While Mr. Mandela, affectionately called Madiba, eventually came out of apartheid jail to lead multiracial South Africa as its first elected president, Sobukwe and several other black nationalist leaders of that country had died; some of them died in apartheid prisons and detention centers (including Steve Biko) as confirmed in the deliberations of the phenomenal South African Truth Commission that unraveled details of some of the inhumane activities of agents of the apartheid regime, including how some anti-apartheid exiles were chased and maimed or killed with parcel bombs. Among them was Ruth First (who was killed in her office at Edourado Mondlane University in Maputo, Mozambique). Ms. First, beloved wife of Joe Slovo, comes readily to mind because when one of us (as coauthors) worked for *Africa magazine*, ably edited and published by Dr. Ralph Uwuechue, one of Nigeria's excellent former diplomats, I remember occasionally working on submissions from Ms. First for our magazine. We were very happy that we had the honor of assigning Alan Wieder's excellent biographical publication, *Ruth First and Joe Slovo in the War Against Apartheid*, to be reviewed by the journals that we served as book review editors.

A.B. always remembers a telephone conversation that he had with Ms. First in the early 1970s in the offices of *Africa Magazine.* She mentioned how she came to the United Kingdom as a new exile from South Africa in 1964. Eventually, she decided to leave and go to Mozambique, where she initially accepted the position of a director of a research program for training at Universidade Eduardo Mondlane (or Eduardo Mondlane University) in the Mozambican capital of Maputo. Sadly, on August 17, 1982, she opened a letter bomb, sent to her at the university from the South African police's then deadly special branch, and she was killed instantly. Before that, she had been able to tell her story of her arrest and detention by the same South African special branch in 1963; that episode was the result of her 1965 book, *117 Days*. As she mentioned in the conversation—like mother like daughter—one of her children (Gillian Slovo) also published her memoir in 1977, titled *Every Secret Thing: My Family, My Country.*

In retrospect, one could only conjecture the euphoric welcome that Malcolm X, if he were alive, would have extended to Madiba (as Mr. Nelson Mandela is also called) during his post-prison tour of the United

States. Although Dr. King did not live to witness the historic moment, it was simply wonderful that his widow, Coretta Scott King, represented him well when Mr. Mandela and Mrs. Winnie Mandela—whom Mrs. King had supported—paid a courtesy visit to the King Center for Nonviolent Social Change on Auburn Avenue in Atlanta, Georgia. It is a known fact to both of us, who variously served the King Papers Project (now a major research institute or center) at Stanford University or at the King Center that, indeed, when Mandela was still imprisoned, Mrs. King communicated with his former wife, Winnie, on a regular basis. She also sent a variety of gifts to her by mail, for which Winnie always expressed gratitude; some of these events, which took place within the context of genuine Pan-Africanism on the part of Mrs. King, are to be discussed in a comparative biographical study of the dignified widow of the slain civil rights leader that many admirers saw as the first lady of the U.S. civil rights movement.

THE PERSISTENT CONCERNS OF MALCOLM X

In all, Malcolm X paid three consecutive visits to African countries, but that of 1964 was the most extensive, as he spent almost half a year on the continent, as underscored earlier. During all of the visits, he tried to observe lifestyles as well as the social-*cum*-economic circumstances of the citizens that he encountered. In fact, regardless of some of the shortcomings Malcolm X detected, which made the impoverished populace of several countries appear unprogressive, he was proud of the fat that most of the countries were ruled by their own black leaders. That was something that he found to be lacking in the United States for black people anywhere they lived, even if they happened to be in the majority. What Malcolm X had noticed, instead, was that even where blacks happened to be in the majority in some cities, blacks would only be prompted to help in electing white mayors and predominantly white council members and leaders, including chairpersons.

Of course, the famous joke, over the years, was that it was when a city was either about to die off or to declare bankruptcy (as happened recently in Detroit) that a black person would be catapulted into a leadership position, as a mayor or chairman of the city council. It is very important to discuss some of the major issues that Malcolm X, Dr. King, Carmichael (Kwame Ture), and other black leaders harped on, which still persist, even if some African countries that Malcolm so much admired are also mired in their own miseries.

For varied reasons, Malcolm X cheered African countries for attaining their independence as well as black leadership positions, but loathed those that, at the time, still swam in colonialism and neo-colonialism. In fact, Malcolm was aware of some of the patriotic and radical slogans of leaders like Nkrumah and Toure, who preferred self governance in poverty to wallowing in riches while in servitude; they also made it clear to European powers controlling their respective nations (Ghana and Guinea) that they preferred independence with danger over servitude with tranquility. As president of Ghana Kwame Nkrumah often harped on with the slogan that African nations deserved the right to attain independence and, thereafter, to govern or misgovern themselves. Malcolm X did embrace such slogans in whole because he himself could not tolerate dominance from whites, not even in the United States, where they were supposed to be in the majority.

Several of the U.S. civil rights leaders, whose supporters had different interpretations of national events, included Dr. King, Malcolm X, and Stokely Carmichael (Kwame Ture). They also included the black supporters of the movement that Dr. King, in his 1964 Nobel acceptance lecture, referred to as the foot soldiers of his movement. However, Dr. King and the other civil rights' leaders did not think that most of the ills and economic shortcomings that they were battling for or fighting against on American streets, through non-violent protests, would still persist in the latter part of the twentieth century and up to the twenty-first century. Sadly, they do!

However, blacks and other racial minorities of today continue to witness those sad odysseys in the day-to-day activities of the middle class and the downtrodden about whom leaders of civil rights organizations bemoaned. In a brilliant analysis of the plight of U.S. black men and women, professors Charles Johnson and John McCluskey, Jr., both distinguished writers, have confirmed the obviously sad situation in their co-edited book, *Black Men Speaking*, published in 1996 by Indiana University Press. They contended that when soliciting manuscripts from contributors, they asked them to discuss the problems or crises confronting black people, especially the black male. According to the co-editors, their contributors were responding to what was regarded as a crisis in the black community in general, but that "the problem has obviously become more acute than before, if the barrage of egregious statistics about black America is to be believed" (Johnson and McCluskey 1996, ix). These award-winning authors went on to point out that, in 1989, "one out of four young black men was entering, within, or emerging from the criminal justice system. In 1995, that number increased to one out of three" (Johnson and McCluskey 1996; ix). The co-editors further quoted the NAACP Legal Defense and Educational Fund:

> On the average day in the United States, thirty-one black people are murdered -- one every forty-six minutes. Homicide remains the leading cause of death for black males ages fifteen to nineteen. More Blacks are murdered every six weeks in America than were lynched during the last 110 years... (Johnson and McCluskey 1996)

According to *Black Men Speaking*, the statistical data get worse, thereby adding *inter alia*: "One of ten Black Americans was the victim of a violent crime in 1995. A Justice Department survey conducted among 110,000 households reported that among blacks twelve or older, 111 of every 1,000 were victims of a violent crime; a rate 25 percent higher than whites..." (Johnson and McCluskey 1996, x). In fact, the statistics get worse when it comes to unemployment among black and other minority youths, as well as the rate of those in American prisons. These were among the disturbing pieces of information that Malcolm X, Dr. King, Carmichael (later called Toure), Congressman John Lewis, and other civil rights stalwarts were fighting hard to help ameliorate, at least to bring dignity to their people.

Carrying out our own research activities and publications, we have catalogued several aspects of black-on-black crime, ethnic chauvinism, or outright racism that in Africa (where Malcolm X visited for several months in 1964) is labelled as tribalism. We have also documented twenty-first century frictions between continental Africans and African Americans, of which Malcolm, King, and other civil rights leaders would not be proud. In *Black and Multiracial Politics*, professors Alex-Assensoh and Lawrence J. Hanks collaborated with contributors to discuss some of the black and multiracial conflicts and efforts at collaboration. For the book, a contribution from then Indiana University professor A.B. Assensoh (now professor emeritus and co-author of this book) is in Chapter 6, and it is titled "Conflict or Cooperation?: Africans and African-Americans in Multiracial America." The essay highlights some of the thorny issues and irritating nuances on both sides of the racial spectrum when it comes to continental Africans and diaspora-based blacks (African Americans). It is shown, however, that just as Malcolm X would have wanted, when it comes to the ethos of nationalism and civil rights, the pendulum swings toward cooperation between the two groups. It is further demonstrated in the chapter that, over the years, there was transparent collaboration, as well as cooperation, between continental Africans and African Americans, who were referred to in the days of yore as negroes. While sociology professor E. Franklin Frazier of Howard University and a few of his black intellectual friends saw no African influences in their lives and on their scholarship, Dr. DuBois and other Pan-Africanists saw it differently. The chapter points out that not only did Dr. DuBois live in Africa, attain Ghanaian citizenship, and also die and was buried there in 1963, the year that Dr. King led the historic march on Washington, Du Bois also became the founding editor of the *Encyclopedia Africana* in order to "document African culture and history" (Alex-Assensoh and Hanks 2000, 116).

1965: The Year of the Assassination of Malcolm X

In his "Drum Major Instinct" speech of February 4, 1968, as well as the "I Have Been to the Mountain Top" speech of April 1968, Dr. King, as Malcolm's fellow civil rights activist and leader, predicted his own death, while making it abundantly clear that he was not afraid to die. Although Malcolm X did frankly make it obvious that he could easily be a target, he did not do or say anything to indicate the possibility of dying in his prime.

However, close associates of Malcolm X did have the inkling that staying in Africa from April to November 1964 was part of his strategy to elude his plotters, who would eventually conspire, plot, and go after him in the Audubon Ballroom in February 1965. His wife, Betty, was pregnant when her husband was embarking on his African trip in 1964, but she was not worried because she knew that it would be good for Malcolm to hold court and subsequently break bread with his fellow Africans. Since he could not live in Africa forever, Malcolm X returned to America in November of 1964 and, three months later, on February 21, 1965, he was dead at the hands of alleged hired assassins.

Very interestingly, however, some of the close NOI associates of Malcolm X did know that and, as he described it sometimes, he was a "walking dead" man. One of them was his own mentee, Nation of Islam leader Louis Farrakhan, who admitted in a 60 Minutes CBS interview that his incendiary rhetoric could have played a role in the 1965 assassination of the civil rights leader. Mr. Farrakhan reportedly made the admission to Malcolm X's daughter, Attallah Shabazz, and CBS Correspondent Mike Wallace. Mr. Farrakhan did not admit active participation in the plot or the assassination; instead he, among other details, said: "I may have been complicit in words that I spoke leading up to February 21 [1965]." In addition, Farrakhan told Shabazz and Wallace: "I acknowledge that and regret that if any word that I have said caused the loss of life of a human being." Later on, Ms. Shabazz issued a statement thanking Mr. Farrakhan for acknowledging his role, and concluded by saying: "I wish him peace."

Among those who would have also known ahead of time that Malcolm X was an assassination target were individuals directly involved in the dastardly act, including Thomas Hagan, described as the shotgun-toting assassin. When being paroled in 2010 for his role in the assassination forty-five years earlier, it was stated that, he shot "the charismatic activist as his pregnant wife and daughters watched in horror." At sixty-nine years old, Hagan left the Lincoln Correctional Facility in Harlem, New York. He was described as one of the three men convicted in the Feb. 21, 1965, assassination of Malcolm X. As a member of the Nation of Islam, he was called Talmadge X Haver, who was sentenced to twenty years to life for the killing of Malcolm X in front of four hundred Islamic followers. In retrospect, one wonders why a member of NOI, which Malcolm helped to build into a formidable religious group, would want to have Malcolm X assassinated. The answer might not be too difficult to find; I note the following: the New York police investigators claimed that some of the NOI leaders were very high on the list of possible plotters and hit men, who were involved in the Audubon Ballroom killing of such a formidable black leader.

The Malcolm X assassination investigation went on to recall that, in 1964, Malcolm X revealed publicly that Elijah Mohammed, the leader of the Nation of Islam (NOI), was guilty of impregnating several of his teenage secretaries, which was in direct violation of his own preaching against sex outside of marriage. Malcolm and others brought to the American public consciousness the fact that the NOI leader (Elijah Muhammad) allegedly had eight children with his first wife, Clara Muhammad, whom he had reportedly married in 1917. He also reportedly had three children with Lucille Rosary Muhammad, one child with Evelyn Muhammad, and four children with Tvnnetta Muhammad. Malcolm X also claimed that Muhammad was rumored to have fathered several children from other female relationships, counting not less than twenty-one children for the Honorable Elijah Muhammad. Indeed, Malcolm X and the other disaffected leaders in the Nation of Islam, who chose to follow him, were very indignant that Muhammad, as they alleged, used the NOI funds to support his many children and his concubines, including children from his nuclear family.

Malcolm X and his supporters were vindicated at the end of Elijah Muhammad's life in Chicago, when, upon the NOI leader's death, nineteen of his children allegedly filed lawsuit for benefits from his estate and for recognition as heirs to Muhammad's fortunes by the World Community of Islam, which had succeeded NOI. Malcolm X's antagonism of Muhammad, who was very powerful at the time, was apparent. Therefore, it did not surprise many Americans that his assassination could be shrouded in such mystery and that those who were highly suspected to be involved could escape justice. Like several other American assassinations, the investigation of the death of Malcolm X produced only Hagan and two convicted blacks as the perpetrators, who had their day in court and were eventually found guilty and sentenced to terms of imprisonment. Still, the public is of the opinion that, like the enigma that the victim himself was, the real plotters behind Malcolm's assassination have been shielded to this day. Whether that is true or not, several of these black men have died with their secrets buried with them.

Given the foregoing circumstances and the manner in which Malcolm X was killed, many of his African admirers were sad that he did not remain permanently on the continent during his long 1964 sojourn there. In their opinion, no assassin could have crossed the Atlantic Ocean to Africa in order to maim or eliminate Malcolm X as was done on February 21, 1965, when he was getting ready to address a mammoth rally of his beloved Muslim Mosque, Inc. (MMI) and the Organization of Afro-American unity (OAAU) Islamic group.

The warm African sentiments toward Malcolm X from African sources were very genuine because his African cousins, as some people referred to continental Africans, knew that although Malcolm X and his fellow blacks lived in and earned their keep from America, many of them still had spiritual and sentimental attachments to the African continent. It was therefore natural to find support for this assertion from Professor Gaines, who wrote that in 1964, as OAAU and MMI leader, Malcolm urged his fellow African Americans to continue to live in America, but should "migrate to Africa culturally, philosophically, and spiritually" (Gaines 2006, 205).

It was a fact that Malcolm X's critics did their best to present him in a negative light. Yet, during his lifetime, Malcolm X was viewed positively and progressively by his fellow African Americans, who migrated to Ghana in their efforts to either accept or embrace the late President Nkrumah's 1951 Lincoln University commencement address appealing to U.S.-based Blacks to return to the future Ghana that he would head as the first indigenous leader, especially following her freedom from the British in 1957.

The aim of the many African Americans, who left American shores for Ghana in West Africa, was mainly to help rebuild the motherland. That was why upon his assassination there was an outpouring of true compassion for him and his family in and outside the United States. For example, on February 24, 1965, barely three days after Malcolm's assassination, Julian Mayfield, one of his very strong African American allies living in Ghana, wrote a very passionate eulogy that was published in several press circles in the African country. To Mayfield, all men and women of African descent globally had suffered what he considered to be a grievous loss. Malcolm X was seen as working with Dr. King and other black leaders to achieve the same end for their people through different tactics. However, Mayfield, like other Malcolm X admirers, felt that the slain black Islamic leader "was the only Afro-American [African-American] leader of national stature, who sought to unify Africa with its descendants in the Western hemisphere and who also rejected an accommodating attitude and non-violence" (Gaines 2006, 206).

What was also very interesting at that time was that several Americans and non-Americans, who saw Malcolm X as mellowing after his pilgrimage to Mecca, wondered why he would be so brutally eliminated from the American political and religious scene. That was also why

Mayfield, in his February 24, 1965, write-up honoring Malcolm X's memory in the Ghanaian press, did not mince words when he wrote that in his eyes, Malcolm's "uncompromising stands [on several issues] made him the most dangerous man in America" (Gaines 2006, 206).

According to Professor Gaines, the Ghana-based African American writer (Mayfield) drew lessons from the life of Malcolm that would resonate well with the political culture of Ghanaian society that had been weakened by malfeasance, adding, "Malcolm was honest, incorruptible, a man with a ready smile" (Gaines 2006, 206).

It was also revealed after Malcolm's death that Africa, for various reasons, meant a lot to Malcolm X. In correspondence with his Africa-based friends, he had asked that certain wishes be fulfilled for him, if anything happened to him later in life back in America. "Malcolm had written to Mayfield, expressing his wish, in the event of his death, that some African state [nation] would give refuge to his wife and children" (Gaines 2006, 206).

From all indications, Africa meant so much to Malcolm X that his trips and stay there—similar to his journeys to the Islamic Holy Land in the Middle East—transformed his life. Although he variously disagreed with Dr. King's non-violence philosophy in the face of violence against black men and women during non-violent protests in America's southern cities, it has now been shown, beyond any reasonable doubt, that at the time of Malcolm X's assassination, he wanted to avoid all traces of violence around him. That was why, among varied details, as Columbia University professor Manning Marable wrote: "Despite the recent firebombing and the escalating threats of violence, Malcolm had resisted the carrying of arms by his security team that Sunday with the sole exception of Reuben [at the OAAU meeting at which he was assassinated]" (Marable 2012, 5).

Indeed, Malcolm X's life journey raised queries that aligned well with what Countee Cullen touched on in his celebrated poem, "What is Africa to me." Cullen, the African American poet with a stature similar to that of Langston Hughes and others, was a leading figure in the historic Harlem

Renaissance. He used his poetic genius to show the connection between Africa and her lost sons and daughters in the American diaspora. In fact, in a 1940 autobiography titled *Dusk of Dawn*, the legendary Dr. W.E.B. DuBois made sure to include Cullen's poem, as he himself asked, "What is Africa to me?" In the book, *W.E.B. DuBois on Africa*, Professors Provenzo and Abaka also wrote that they approached the answer to the question by endeavoring to assemble "many of DuBois' original writings on Africa and to add not only commentary and background to them, but a large interpretative discussion in our Introduction" (Provenzo and Abaka 2012, i). Similarly, we have sought to provide this brief but purposeful study of Malcolm X's connections with his beloved Africa as a way of answering a query about what, indeed, Africa was and means to Malcolm X and his descendants.

A.B. Assensoh, LLM, PhD,
Yvette M. Alex-Assensoh, PhD, JD,
Eugene, Oregon, USA

Acknowledgments

This book's origins are partly from the Indiana University course that we successfully and enthusiastically co-taught for the prestigious Indiana University Department of Political Science on the Reverend Dr. Martin Luther King, Jr. and Malcolm X, who was also known in life as El-Hajj Malik El-Shabazz (the title he acquired upon completing the important Islamic pilgrimage to Mecca in the Middle East). Therefore, his wife (Betty) and his six daughters added the Shabazz surname to their names.

In fact, the political science course for Indiana University upper-level students of junior or senior rank had its own odyssey, as it was introduced and regularly taught in the department by one of its excellent black scholars, Professor Lawrence J. Hanks (also known as Dr. Lawrence Julius Hanks, Sr., the Harvard University-educated political scientist, who is one of those for whom this publication is dedicated. He honed his skills to become an excellent motivational speaker). Unfortunately, for the Fall 2011 semester, Professor Hanks was so ill that it became apparent that he could not teach the course. That was why Professor Russell Hanson, the chairman of the department and a distinguished political scientist himself, invited both of us to teach the course.

We had very heavy hearts, as we unfortunately had to replace our dear friend and colleague (Professor Hanks), who sadly passed away in Bloomington, Indiana as a result of his advanced cancerous illness. We were satisfied that he received a very beautiful funeral planned and executed by his nuclear family (led elegantly by Mrs. Diane Hanks, his widow, as well as their children) and several of his Indiana University colleagues and friends. The funeral service in Indiana Memorial Union auditorium, attended by his siblings from Georgia and other U.S. cities, was filled to capacity. Subsequently, he was buried at a cemetery in his Fort Gaines home in Georgia, where his parents and other family members had earlier been interred.

To honor his memory, we were ready to teach the course that he had introduced. Apart from our expertise in political science and history respectively at the time we taught the course, our collaborative credentials included having coauthored scholarly articles and an entire book, *African Military History and Politics, From 1900-Present*, published in 2001 by Palgrave-Macmillan of St. Martin's Press of New York. My own credentials also stem from my extensive research and work on Dr. King and the U.S. civil rights moment, including my earlier book, *Rev. Dr. Martin Luther King, Jr. and America's Quest for Racial Integration*, published by a British publishing company, which was originally part of my postdoctoral studies in the Department of Peace Studies at the University of Bradford in West Yorkshire, United Kingdom.

Furthermore, both of us served in a variety of capacities for the Stanford University-based Martin Luther King, Jr. Papers Project, which is now a major research institute; Yvette was a graduate student intern at Stanford University from The Ohio State University, while A.B. served the project as director of research and associate editor on the Palo Alto campus of Stanford University before he was transferred to the Martin Luther King, Jr. Center for Non-Violent Social Change on Auburn Avenue, Atlanta, Georgia, in similar capacities or positions. There, A.B. worked directly with the office of Mrs. Coretta Scott King and had the pleasure of occasionally helping with drafts of Mrs. King's speeches and her nationally syndicated newspaper columns (interestingly, Mrs. King was never a non-active columnist herself as she would discuss in detail what she wanted in write-ups for her column, including relevant King quotes that she wanted interspersed before one sat down to draft a column that, upon submitting to him through Steve, his research assistant, she also took time to edit).

With all of the foregoing backgrounds, we decided that completing a book about Malcolm X would be auspicious so that if we were to teach a course about Malcolm X, King, or both of them together, we should be able to rely on it. While coauthoring the book on Malcolm X's continental African connections, several colleagues in our respective departments at Indiana University and elsewhere offered support and encouragement. In particular, professor Valerie Grim, A.B.'s African-American and African Diaspora Studies Department's chairperson, during each academic year prodded him on by inquiring about the book's progress as part of the annual Faculty Research Summary (FSR) report. In Yvette's department, successive chairpersons, including professors Jeff Isaacs and Russell ("Russ") Hanson also wanted to know how the work was progressing on the book.

Instead of completing the book, we received an unexpected invitation from Greenwood Publishing Company, an imprint of ABC-CLIO, LLC of Santa Barbara, California to write a biography of Malcolm X, with a promise of a royalty advance, our second such upfront monetary reward (similar to the offer by Palgrave-Macmillan for our 2001 coauthored book); we halted this book project, embarked on the research for the biography, and in the fall of 2011 completed the book titled *Malcolm X: A Biography*, which happens to be part of the Greenwood Biographies Series. We eventually decided to return to the Malcolm X and Africa project as part of a major black leadership project, for which A.B. received Indiana University's competitive Emeritus Professor Research Grant to supplement funding from Yvette's own research funds at the University of

Oregon. We are grateful to the Office of the Vice-Provost for Research at Indiana University. Professors Samuel Gyasi Obeng (Director of African Studies Program at Indiana University) and Professor Grim wrote strongly in support of my application for the grant, and we are grateful!

At the University of Oregon, both of us have distinct portfolios: A.B. serves as Courtesy Emeritus Professor in the History Department as well as a Students' Mentor for the Office of the Vice-Provost for International Affairs, while Yvette holds the substantive positions of Vice-President for Equity and Inclusion and Professor of Political Science. In fact, the 400-level political science course on King and Malcolm X that was assigned for us to co-teach in the Department of Political Science at the University of Oregon did provide additional opportunity for both of us to acquire additional materials for the Malcolm X book project, which is distinctively about his relationship with Africa and aspects of his Islamic religious activities, and which happened to be of interest to his African Muslim brothers and sisters. For that we are eternally grateful to professor Priscilla Southwell, department head of the Political Science Department. A.B. is also very grateful to former dean Scott Coltrane, who is now interim president of the university; he received him warmly and helped arrange a meeting with professor John Cole (then head of the History Department), to see what A. B. could do for the department.

As Professor Cole stepped down to devote more time to his research and other professional interests, Professor Herman took over as the new head of the University of Oregon's History Department; she made sure that, in the Spring 2015 term, A.B. (given his expertise) would teach a 400-level course on Malcolm X, Dr. King, and Africa for the History Department.

A.B. is also grateful to UO Law School dean Michael Moffit as well as LLM Degree Program director Kristie Gibson for the admission to complete a graduate degree in law (LLM). Professor Ibrahim Gassama, John Bonine, Eric Priest, and Jared Margilo contributed to A.B.'s intellectual awareness as their student in a variety of courses (including dean Michael Moffitt, who taught A.B. a "J" Term Settlement Law course). Professor Bonine's coauthored Human Rights and Environment Law course textbook is cited and acknowledged in the references of this book because it was very helpful to us as coauthors.

We are also grateful to colleagues in the Office of International Affairs at University of Oregon, especially vice-provost Dennis Galvan as well as His Excellency Eric Benjaminson ("H.E. EB" to us), a former U.S. ambassador to the Republic of Gabon, who is serving as a director in the Office of International Affairs; Lady Nancy O'Brien, who superbly coordinates work in the office for all of us (we have honorifically given her the title of "Lady" because of the professional way that she carries herself); our colleagues in the African Studies Program at the University of Oregon have also been collegial in extending research and meeting invitations.

Furthermore, we are very grateful to two intellectual colleagues: professor Damien Ejigiri, dean of the Graduate School at Southern University in Baton Rouge, Louisiana, a scholar in his own right who wrote the foreword to this book; he agreed to write the foreword when he was preparing to travel to Makerere University in Uganda, where he serves in an adjunct faculty capacity. We are also grateful to professor Richard W. Hull of the History Department at New York University (NYU) and A.B.'s dissertation director at NYU who, as a true scholar, encouraged us in varied ways when we were completing this book; he saw that the book was important for us to complete for publication. The writing of the publication's introduction fell on the intellectual generosity of Mr. Ivor Agyeman-Duah, who is currently research associate of the University of Oxford's African Studies Center in the UK.

Mr. Agyeman-Duah, who was at the time of writing the introduction a PhD candidate, is the important biographer of Ghana's former president John Agyekum Kufuor. His 394-page biography is titled *Between Faith and History: A Biography of J.A. Kufuor,* and it is published by the United Kingdom-based Ayebia Clarke Publishing Limited. His biography was one of the lauded textbooks for leadership aspects of seminar courses we taught at Indiana University's African American and African Diaspora Studies (AAADS) Department. Mr. Agyeman-Duah is also the founder of the Ghana-based public policy organization, Center for Intellectual Renewal, which famously deals with issues of communication, culture, and economic development.

Apart from Mr. Agyeman-Duah serving in advisory capacities for the World Bank Institute on African Diaspora as well as The Andrew Mellon Foundation of New York on its African program known as Ithaka Aluka, we are happy to underscore that we knew him as a top diplomat of Ghana, with the rank of minister counselor for information, when he invited both of us to team up with distinguished history professor David Owusu-Ansah of the Virginia-based James Madison University in the United Kingdom program observing Ghana's fiftieth independence anniversary (known as Ghana @ 50). As a result, we travelled with our two young sons to London as the host of the Ghana High Commission and took active part as panelists on several events at the School of Oriental and African Studies.

Furthermore, we are most certainly grateful to Mr. Jimmy and Mrs. Angeli Brooks of the University of Oregon as well as Dr. Eric and Dr. (Mrs.) Fese Mokube, and their wonderful children. Similarly, Kenyan-born Dr. Jane Irungu and her very dear husband, Dr. John Irungu Kirika and their children (especially Polly), as well, deserve mention because A.B. has had the opportunity to communicate with them as true scholars and fellow continental Africans, while Yvette works daily in the same University of Oregon Division of Equity and Inclusion, where Yvette is the vice-president and also serving as professor of political science (Dr. Jane Irungu, who was the director of Center for Multicultural Academic Excellence, CMAE, is now the assistant vice-president in the division); in fact, discussions with the Irungus helped when we researched Malcolm X's Kenyan connections, as they remembered from existing literary sources that Malcolm X visited their East African home country.

We are, above all, grateful to our own very close family members: Mrs. Thelma Coleman Alex, Yvette's mother, and A.B.'s mother-in-law, who was visiting us when we were completing the manuscript for the book and had the opportunity to let us know about how Malcolm X was viewed in his lifetime by her and her fellow southerners of the American South, including her late husband, Reverend Livingston Alex, who was for thirty-nine years the pastor of Bethlehem Baptist Church of Breaux Bridge, Louisiana and a regular preacher on and supporter of the civil rights movement that Malcolm and Dr. King were known to have been associated with in the late 1950s and the mid-1960s before their respective assassinations; and teenage sons, Kwadwo Stephen Alex-Assensoh and Livingston Kwabena Alex Assensoh, for their support and enthusiasm for the book projects that we have been working on, and there are indeed several of them! Happily, this book is dedicated to all of them as well.

Also, since 2016 marks seven years since the tragic passing of Dr. Tajudeen Abdul-Raheem in a Kenya road auto accident, he is also warmly memorialized on the dedication page. We as well acknowledge the tremendous moral and intellectual support of Dr. Ama Biney of London, UK, and her family, as Sister Ama (so affably called always) was a great e-mail "conversationalist" in varied ways. Her support included forwarding excellent articles about Malcolm X and other relevant topics to us in Oregon; she is an author in her own right, as her seminal 247-page work on Ghana's late president Kwame Nkrumah, titled *The Political And Social Thought of Kwame Nkrumah,* did remind us that Pan-Africanism, to which Malcolm X adhered, was still a valid factor in studying important leaders, who were actively involved in its practice and promotion.

Sadly, as we were writing the book, professor Ali A. Mazrui passed away. Our dear Mwalimu, who also had a royal Ghanaian title of Nana and his dear wife (Lady Pauline) and children were like members of our own extended family circle. Mwalimu Mazrui, whose encouragement knew no bounds or limitations, is warmly remembered! We always remember the active role he played as our mentor and passionate intellectual listener, with a unique sense of humor, whenever we needed a great mind to share ideas; we were exceedingly happy that the authentic Ghana Kente cloth piece that we gave him as a birthday gift became a trademark, as he wore it almost everywhere at public functions until he passed away. May he rest in peace!

We are especially very thankful to authors and publishers, on whose shoulders we have stood through quotations of their pioneering published works; in thanking them effusively; we also laud them with no limitation, as we found their works very useful to rely on and document as well.

Finally, but certainly not the least, we are grateful to several other cousins, nephews, nieces, siblings, and other family members who encouraged us in a variety of ways. They include attorney Joslyn Renee Alex of Breaux Bridge, Louisiana; Dr. Victor and Mrs. Ophelia Essien as well as Awuraa Bernice (Rabby), Kwabby and Alana of New Jersey; Dr. Herman and Mrs. Vida M. Kwansa as well as Dr. Albert Kwansa and attorney Victor Kwansa (Nana Yaw); Temple University professor emeritus Abu S. and Naana (Mrs.) Abarry; Papa Gyasi as well as Bother Akwasi and Afia Owusu-Ansah; "Alhaji" Hassan Wahab; Mannan, together with his wonderful wife (Nana Ama) and baby Ameer Wahab of Illinois; Computer Engineer Stephen and Mrs. Sophia Agyepong (a wonderful registered nurse) as well as the adoring children, Mr. Yaw Osei Agyepong (a computer engineer in his own right) and Miss Adwoa Agyepong of University of Georgia in Athens, Georgia, all of Powder Springs, Georgia; Professor Harcourt and Dr. Christina Fuller of Georgia State University in Atlanta, Georgia; and their little princesses. Thanks also go to professor Samuel Kojo and Mrs. Sharon Andoh and the family's little princess Rachel of Camden, Connecticut; Mrs. Adwoa Berko (Mama Gloria) as well as Mr. Osei (son-in-law) and the wonderful grandchildren they have given us: Mr. Frank Ocran (an employee of Enterprise Car Rental Company) as well as Ms. Cynthia Tetteh (a pharmacy student of University of Connecticut), and young Jessica, who reads anything that she can lay her hands on from us in Oregon; and gratitude also goes finally for received extended family support, as we were hectically trying to complete the manuscript, from the following as well: Dr. Eric Ofori Bekoe (Brother Kofi) and Nana Kesewaa Ofori-Bekoe, their young princess Nhyira and prince Kwabena Bekoe; and, indeed, accountant Kwabena and Mrs. Kankam as well as Nana Ama Kankam and her siblings, all of Toledo, Ohio.

At this juncture, before we celebrate the positive relationship that has emerged between our publisher, our series editor, and us, it is important to thank the African Union for its permission for us to quote in the appendices the charter of their organization, at least for readers to see and compare it with that of Malcolm X's Association of African-American Unity (OAAU). We deliberately post it because such a comparison is both relevant and healthy.

Meanwhile, we are eternally grateful to Cambria Press and the series editor, professor Toyin Falola, and all other copyeditors, who saw the manuscript through the publication stage. Above all, if there is indeed any correction needed to be done in this book (and we hope not!), we—as coauthors—bear the fullest responsibility of ensuring that future editions of the book will correct any such shortcoming(s)! We have tried to be as objective as possible. However, we have endeavored to make sure that accuracy is the hallmark of the core of this manuscript because of our familiarity with and admiration for "Brother" Malcolm and his family!

A.B. A. & Y.M. A.A.

Malcolm X and Africa

MALCOLM X, PAN-AFRICANISM, AND TODAY'S BLACKS

Ivor Agyeman-Duah

The legacy of Malcolm X's dramatic life and activism evokes different emotional responses in people in the United States of America and also elsewhere: for example, within the United States of America, whose citizen Malcom X was and to whose African American community he belonged, he was seen by his critics as an abrasive witness as well as (in the estimation of his admirers) a victim of racial afflictions, challenges of identity and daily deprivations of the community in which he lived and worked. For example, in Harlem, New York as well as the Deep South —whose plantation economies and general economic growth had been sustained with slave labor of the horrendous transatlantic journey of slavery and enslavement—had been his point of argumentation.

INVOCATION OF W.E.B. DuBois

Slavery and its consequences either partly defined America's democracy or tested its spirit as much as the evolution of aspects of its cuisine, including rice farming in the Carolinas and the music of Negro spirituals; these are events that have been amply documented by the distinguished history professor Claude A. Clegg III in his thoughtful book, *The Price of Liberty: African Americans and the Making of Liberia*, which is about black enslavement in the Carolinas as well as the departure of manumitted American slaves in the mid-1820s for Liberia in West Africa, whose capital of Monrovia was named by the arriving freed slaves (who eventually called themselves Americo-Liberians) to honor the memory of the late American President James Monroe, who lived between 1758 and 1831 and served as the fifth American President (Clegg 2007).

Most certainly, it is the foregoing history, which prompted the legendary Dr. William Edward Burghardt (W. E. B.) DuBois (1868-1963) to ask poetically in 1909 in anger and also with urgency the following:

> Your country, How come it's yours? Before the pilgrims landed, we were here. Here we have brought our three gifts and mingled them with yours; a gift of story and soft-soft, stirring melody to all ill-harmonized and unmelodious land, the gift of sweat and brawn to beat the wilderness, conquer the soil, lay the foundation of the vast, economic empire two hundred years before your weak hands could have done it, the third a gift of the spirit...Our toil, our cheer...Would America have been America without her Negro?" (W.E.B. DuBois 1909).

This historical query also evoked stronger anger after the Second World War, indeed from the 1940s. The leaders of this inherited anger —whether of the small educated black leadership of mixed liberal and revolutionary types, i.e. Du Bois, Frederick Douglass, Marcus Garvey, Elijah Mohammed, Martin Luther King Jr., Malcolm X, Harriet Wilson, Rosa Parks, James Baldwin, Richard Wright, and others—had sought solidarity among continental African leadership and the continent in itself long before the dawn of decolonization and after. Ghana's independence in 1957, for example, created a base although, as world history beckons, Liberia and Haiti have variously been seen as the two oldest black republics. Was there a way Africa's decolonization could help create dignity for African Americans through moral pressure and to ameliorate Africa's role in slavery? Was it a role that had created the African presence in the first place and, later, a factor in America's civil war? These are questions in which Marcus Garvey as well as Malcolm X, the Rev. Dr. Martin Luther King, Jr., and other black leaders of the diaspora before and even after them were interested.

When Kwame Nkrumah—the leader of government business from 1954 and as Ghana's first elected indigenous prime minister in 1957 until his overthrow in a *coup d'etat* in February 1966—asked African Americans in a commencement address of his *alma mater* (Lincoln University in Pennsylvania) for their skills in nation building, was it a formal request or fusion between the practicalities of political Pan-Africanism and the momentum of the U.S. civil rights movement in the United States? Definitely, slavery in the Americas had created dislocated voices among black leadership as to what strategies to adopt in the post-slavery era and integration: Marcus Garvey's Back-to-Africa movement, DuBois-influenced National Association for the Advancement of Colored People (NAACP), and Martin Luther King, Jr.'s leadership of the second phase of the civil rights movement as well as King's eventual Southern Christian Leadership Conference (SCLC). It had been the same with revolutionary organizations in the decolonization movement in Africa: for example, the Algerian War of Independence, led by the National Liberation Front dating back from 1954; The *Mau Mau* Rebellion in Kenya from 1952 to 1960; wars of the intelligentsia in Ghana, Nigeria, and elsewhere to gain freedom in the late 1950s and the 1960s.

Probably it was for Ghana's multifaceted independence celebrations in early March 1957 that Nkrumah evoked the work of Marcus Garvey as well as that of Casely-Hayford and others, adding that the people of the new Ghana had come to the end of their struggles, especially as Ghana's nationalist struggle for decolonization had been captured as part of Nkrumah's 1957 published memoirs, *Ghana: Autobiography of Kwame Nkrumah*, and also in Professor Harcourt Fuller's London School of Economics' study, published as a recent bok with the enticing titled of *Building The Ghanaian Nation-State: Kwame Nkrumah's Symbolic Nationalism* (Nkrumah 1957; Fuller 2014). A critical acknowledgement of the joint efforts of African American and African leadership, which had been most visible at the Pan-African Conference in Manchester in 1945 (of which Du Bois, Nkrumah, Kenyatta, and Joe Appiah were very active organizers) came to fruition with Ghana's historic March 6, 1957, independence

BOOK'S MAIN FOCUS AND IMPORTANCE

This book on Malcolm X and his African connections provides a detailed account of the extremely relevant Pan-African activism of a figure unavoidable regardless of whether revisionist or narrative history of the times in which he lived is taken—times that were indeed very profound. Indeed, as I have come to know for several years, Professor A. B. Assensoh, the lead author for this well-researched book, is an intellectual adventurer, who witnessed as a professional journalist part of the decolonization of Ghana and other freed West African nations. Later on, in the mid-1960s, he is known to have developed personal contacts with some of the leaders, including the late Nkrumah whom he met in person; he was, in fact, the first Ghanaian journalist to interview him during the late Ghanaian leader's exile years in the Guinean capital of Conakry, where Nkrumah lived between 1966 and 1972 after his overthrow by the combined forces of the military and police of Ghana. Professor Assensoh was at the time editor-in-chief of three Liberian newspapers: *Daily Listener, Saturday Chronicle*, and *Sunday Digest*. Professor Assensoh is known to have reported on Africa in the 1970s and 1980s as a journalist, during which time he focused his journalistic accounts on the activities of the Ethiopia-based Organization of African Unity (or OAU but now known as the African Union or AU). Affably called A.B. by professional colleagues, friends, and his future teachers, he also worked for media outlets in London, United Kingdom, and later on he became a resident correspondent in Stockholm and London, respectively, for *Afriscope Magazine* of Nigeria and *To the Point International Magazine* of South Africa, which was based in Antwerp, Belgium.

Also, I recall very well when Dr. Assensoh (as A.B.) worked as an editor for *Africa magazine* in London, which was edited and published by the former Nigerian diplomat, the late Chief Ralph Uwechue (1935–2014). As a journalist, A.B dealt professionally with African diplomats who were involved in the evolution of Africa's foreign policy. His transition from international journalist to prolific academic confirms his credentials as an Africanist.

Professor Assensoh's co-author, Dr. Yvette M. Alex-Assensoh, as a distinguished academic in her own right, is a full professor and an administrator. She is also the spouse of Professor Assensoh, with whom they have two adorable sons, whom I had the pleasure of first meeting in London, when I served as a diplomat at the Ghana High Commission there. Yvette is an African American political scientist and a licensed lawyer (or attorney), who is endowed with an unlimited knowledge of family memories of the times and the conditions in which Malcolm X lived his life between the mid-1950s and mid-1960s. She is a descendant of manumitted slaves in the United States who, since the 1960s, have emerged as a new well-educated African American class that is formidable in their career pursuits.

The subject of the co-authors' collaborative work includes the use of multiple primary, secondary, and extant materials gathered over the years, with their superb historical and political analyses of the same. They have done it with such precision that it brings Malcolm X's prominence to the fore historically, and they are to be unlimitedly commended.

ACTIVISM OF MALCOLM X

Promptly, one may ask: to what end and meaning was Malcolm X's activism? Or to be more explicit, a follow-up query is this: What was Malcolm X's understanding of Pan-Africanism, or what did Pan Africanism mean to him (Malcolm X)? It is certainly very difficult in categorical terms to try and answer the two foregoing queries for a variety of reasons, including the fact that Malcolm X was viewed differently by many people. He did not, for example, have a solid platform in New York, let alone the entire United States, for his activism; he was also not as grounded as expected in his understanding of the Islamic faith to endear himself to many in mainstream Islam, especially after his conversion, having done so for purely political reasons than for spiritual yearning, and at the prompting of his older brothers. He has discussed this issue in his published memoirs, the latest edition with a foreword by his daughter, Atallah Shabazz (Malcolm X 1987).

Malcolm X, unfortunately, did not have a strong political base in Africa to propagate much of the arguments he had advanced during his visit to the continent. Yet, in this very useful book, the coauthors use their well-delineated substantive chapters to offer readers discussions that call for a delightful engrossment in the issues, and presented in prose as engaging as that found in a good novel. Some of the rich sources utilized were from people who had known Malcolm in Africa and who were known to Dr. A.B. Assensoh as a professional journalist. He and his co-author have pointed out that their access to these personal sources makes for a publication that is objective.

They have written eloquently that they sought to provide a brief but purposeful study of Malcolm X's connections with his beloved Africa —to the continent and also to its people, whom he saw as his kith and kin. It was also a way of answering a query about what, indeed, Africa was and still remains to Malcolm X and his descendants. The coauthors have shown very clearly that Malcolm X had a big heart for Africa. Furthermore, he had a vision for the African-*cum*-African-American relationship, with unity at its core. Therefore, if he had lived beyond February 1965, when he was put to death by an assassin's bullet, he could have utilized, for the benefit of Pan-Africanism, his vast experiences.

Several aspect of this publication capture as well as support, with some solid narrations, actions and details of Malcolm X's work in Africa, especially through his visits to Egypt and, in later travels, during courtesy calls on several modern African leaders: Nkrumah in Ghana and in meetings with various groups at the University of Ghana, where the Ghanaian playwright and poet, Ama Ata Aidoo, still remembers the electrifying speech Malcolm X gave; with Jomo Kenyatta and Tom Mboya in Kenya; in Tanzania with Julius K. Nyerere and his fellow Muslim Babu. He also made contacts, at the United Nations, with some of Africa's top diplomats, including the distinguished Guinean ambassador to the United States, Boubacar Diallo Telli, who became the first secretary-general of the OAU, in addition to Ghana's United Nations Ambassador Alex Quaison-Sackey, the former president of the UN General Assembly.

MALCOLM X's IDEOLOGY AND ANTI-AMERICAN STANCES

Malcolm X's ideological dispositions and methods for achieving his goals, however, made little impact in getting these leaders as individuals or as a collective at the OAU to support his requested public denunciation of the United States. There was no doubt that some of these leaders did understand where Malcolm X was coming from. However, although they had become independent of European colonial rule, they still depended on the erstwhile colonial masters for international developmental assistance. After the Second World War, there was an increasing reliance on U.S. economic assistance and aid, which these new African nations could not do without. These factors were obviously missing in the calculations of Malcolm X, who expected the African leaders to side with him against America and her allies.

The African heads of state that Malcolm X interacted with during his prolonged sojourn on the African continent in 1964 listened to him carefully and, most likely, they also enjoyed his charisma and audacity in taking the new world powers on in his activism. Therefore, they accorded him some diplomatic courtesies. However, ethical dimensions expected of a sovereign country's behavior went against Malcolm X's radical quests. It partly explained why the African leaders at the OAU conference in 1964 in Cairo could not pass any public resolution supporting Malcolm's distributed memorandum, which was highly anti-United States. Sadly, as he said—and has been quoted by the late Columbia University professor Manning Marable—it was not because these leaders had been bought by American dollars (Marable 2011).

It also did not dawn on Malcolm X at the time that historically the U.S. could only be changed from within, and that the American situation that he (Malcolm) did not like could, indeed, be modified from within and in coalition with others with similar ideological dispositions. Also, the new leadership in Africa had fought colonialism with strategies largely from within. Furthermore, Malcolm X's plain speaking on controversial issues did alienate some of the African leaders from his laudable cause of human-rights campaigning. Religious confrontation in comparing the leader of the Nation of Islam, the then Honorable Elijah Mohammed, with biblical prophets was seen as an exaggeration by some African leaders, who were Christians. Rather it incurred the displeasure of many other Christians, who would otherwise have supported his cause. Thus, in as much as the causes of his agitation were understandable, his strategies and negative media reports of his own creation did not help his cause.

What emerged shortly after independence in much of Africa was the transition of political Pan-Africanism to a focus on economic development. As a result, economic cooperation within the OAU itself became stronger, as manifested in the regional economic and currency blocs that would later emerge, including the East African Community (EAC), the Common Markets for Eastern and Southern Africa (COMESA), Economic

Community of West African States (ECOWAS), South African Development Community (SADC), and others. Above all, there was no inkling that Malcolm X was interested in either economic Pan-Africanism or with the belief in Nkrumah's famous slogan: "Seek ye first the political kingdom. and everything else would be added unto thee."

MALCOLM X AND AFRICA'S OPPOSITION LEADERS

My inference from this exciting book is that Malcolm X did not show any serious attempts to befriend the opposition parties, movements, or leaders or to team up with followers in any African country as a way of enlarging either his own cause in particular or that of the African-American situation in general. By the early 1960s, some of the African leaders that he had endeavored to court or befriend had already become dictatorial having created one-party states that undermined basic human rights through preventive detention laws, which were instituted to cripple opposition leaders and their supporters. Also, opponents of such regimes suffered jail sentences without charges or recourse to court appeal. In fact, countries with such capricious laws included Nkrumah's Ghana and Sekou Toure's Guinea. Sadly, the victims were not very different from African American civil rights campaigners killed or jailed in the United States. For example, the Guinean diplomat, former UN Ambassador Diallo Telli, who according to the authors of this book had been so helpful to Malcolm X, was arrested on trumped-up charges, detained, tortured, and died in Sekou Toure's detention center in Guinea without been charged with any crime or tried by any court of law of Guinea.

There have always been leaders of liberation struggles interested in addressing past injustices as a tool of progressive humanity. There are also others who are merely interested in litigation of the past for revenge and egotism. It was interesting when Nigeria's recently elected leader, President Muhammadu Buhari, said in a speech that, for him, the past was a prologue— a statement that enlisted criticism. Similarly, Malcolm X had his own axiomatic stance on life and issues affecting him, whereby he wanted friends in Africa to find refuge on the continent for his wife (Betty) and his five daughters because, as he often predicted, he anticipated a short life; predictably, Malcolm's life was shortened at thirty-nine years old in 1965, when he was assassinated in a hail of assassins' bullets in the Audubon Ballroom, where he was preparing to address a meeting of his newly-formed Organization of Afro-American Unity (OAAU).

As the historical records have so far shown, Malcolm X died litigating on the historic past. He never considered a coalition of the willing, indeed of white and black Americans, who detested the system of inequality in which he lived. His radicalism was such that even the extreme religious organization he adored, the Nation of Islam, had to part ways with him in the end for his reported jubilation in the assassination of U.S. President John F. Kennedy. It is said that Malcolm X allegedly said that the assassination was a mere fact that the chickens were coming home to roost, with this specific statement: "Being an old farm boy myself, chickens coming home to roost never did make me sad; they've always made me glad."

It is possible that if Malcolm X had lived beyond 1965, he might have changed some of his ideological positions, just as he tried to mellow on race after his pilgrimage to Mecca, where he interacted with black and white Muslims. After all, many radical liberation leaders did undergo some political realignment over the years. However, if we are to evaluate history—indeed from the 1950s to the first two decades of the twenty-first century—one can underscore that it was the liberal black class and not the militant revolutionary caucus that had triumphed. There is no denying that Malcolm X raised issues of injustice, of historical wrongs, of brutal racism against African Americans. In fact, the top African diplomat (Dr. Quaison-Sackey) —who many thought would have become the first black UN secretary-general in the 1980s—basically did say in his interview with Professor Assensoh, who was a journalist in the 1990s in Accra, that Malcolm X was a very trustworthy friend who lived a dignified life. He was therefore sorry that the black Muslim leader's detractors often tried to use his earlier police arrests as a yardstick to measure his entire life. To him, they were childhood indiscretions.

However, the leadership Malcolm X sought to give would not be one that could lead to the triumph of African Americans from suppression: what W.E.B. Du Bois had called The Talented Tenth or the Guiding Hundredth, which implies that only with the emergence of exceptional strategies of leadership (one that is inclusive) could blacks, whether in America or Africa, be saved from their afflictions. Marcus Garvey as well as Malcolm X, Louis Farrakhan, and Al Sharpton have defined it differently. To them, there was the need for the massive support of the grassroots for an identified black leader to make a difference in national politics. For example, when it became clear that President Barack H. Obama, as a senator, was a serious contender in the democratic primaries, several prominent black politicians—including the Rev. Jesse Jackson, Sr., and Rev. Al Sharpton and others—believed he could become the U.S. president in the end. These were leaders who had campaigned on black identity and on the history of the past: wanting to gain the U.S. presidency to correct past wrongs.

Even William Julius Wilson, the leading black sociologist at Harvard University, before he crossed the carpet to be with Obama from Hillary Clinton's campaign quarters, did not think so. Yet, Mr. Obama did: he addressed issues affecting Americans without any racial bar, and when he had to talk about race, it was an inclusive American problem that needed a solution from all and sundry. Wilson joined him, so did the then Marxist-Princeton University philosophy professor Cornel West. Incidentally, I have learned over the years that Professor Wilson's research and overall scholarship had a tremendous influenced on coauthor Professor Alex-Assensoh's doctoral dissertation at The Ohio State University, which she later significantly revised and published as a 295-page book, with the title *Neighborhoods, Family, and Political Behavior in Urban America*, which was co-published by Garland Publishing, Inc. (a member of Taylor

& Francis Group) and The Maxine Goodman Levin Center of Cleveland State University (Alex-Assensoh 1998).

CROSSING THE RUBICON

It was surprising that after the Rubicon had been crossed (with Obama's Democratic Party victory speech in Chicago and his Washington D.C. swearing in), the exclusive and furious ideas of Malcolm X emerged among polished but disturbing intellectual juggernauts. Cornel West, for example, became a present-day Malcolm X in a different context, indeed in the same black versus white mood. President Obama, Professor West charged, had neglected African Americans and embraced instead the rich and the powerful who had not supported him, and had thus become what the professor saw as black mascot of Wall Street oligarchs, and as a puppet of corporate plutocrats. He also has seen him as the head of what Dr. West saw as the American killing machine.

Mr. Obama's proverbial price of the ticket to the epoch of that historic day had been worthless in the eyes of West and Fredrick Harris, whose blistering book, *The Price of the Ticket*, had appropriated the master— James Baldwin's book of the same title—as an imputation of Obama's journey. Now, few people in the world would say that President Obama's journey had been worthless, or that he ever fought the election in the name of African American history as few would also tell you that they agree with Malcolm X's memorandum that African leaders of the 1960s should have voted and taken a stance against U.S. domestic policy in relation to the apparent human rights abuses in the U.S. However, one can infer from this book by Professors Assensoh and Alex-Assensoh that, fifty years after the death of Malcolm X, furious arguments, sometimes ideological positions of old that did not help the cause of integration, continue to exist, and that attempts to overlook the achievements of American exceptionalism also persists.

CONCLUSION: MALCOLM X VS. EXTREME RADICALISM

Sometimes one is forced to write off the extremist opinions of the Malcolm X-type or the neo-radical philosopher-type, which could also be the basis of racism, white or black, until one thinks again. The circuitous history of race of the 1950s and the 1960s did come home to roost: Ferguson, Missouri, the Baltimore Riots, Charleston, and South Carolina—they did so on the cheap, resulting in the loss of black lives. It is precisely at this juncture that the anger of Malcolm X emerges rightly again, and the old questions which gnawed at Malcolm X are asked in a variety of ways.

If Malcolm X had been alive and had instigated some of the riots following the death of those blacks today, it would not have been a surprise since it would have been in line with his activism. The fact that these incidents happened fifty years after the death of Malcom X—and concerning matters for which he was angry—is a reminder of the unfinished racial healing in America. The shootings and deaths of blacks from August 2014 to June 2015 are unforgettable, but the act perpetrated by a white youth who shot to death a small praying congregation of nine worshippers at the Emmanuel African Methodist Episcopal Church, including the head Pastor Clementa C. Pinckney, in Charleston, ("a murder in the cathedral") is most memorable.

President Obama, who gave the eulogy at the memorial service of his pastor friend, turned it into a major moving speech on race relations in America. It was the third one of his presidency and, also, the second that touched on African American Christian spirituality. He fell on John Newton, the once wealthy slave merchant, who repented, for support. President Obama sang Newton's *Amazing Grace*, whose penultimate verses are striking:

> Through many dangers toils and snare
> I have already come
> 'Tis grace that brought me safe this far
> And grace will lead me home
> The Lord has promised good to me

His word my hope secures
He will my shield and portion be
As long as life endures.

At the time of the singing by President Obama, we had seen for nine months, shootings and deaths leading to race riots, looting and destruction of property and the biggest solidarity marches across the U.S. since the civil rights era of the 1960s. We also saw in all of these sad incidents, whites as well as blacks, Latinos, and other people of color joining in against a system.

"Tis grace that brought me safe this far, and grace will take me home," Obama sang both as a personal realization of America's advancement in race relations and at the same time, the awaited grace that will further lift race relations in the U.S. to the homestretch. Most certainly, this book is part of the difficult, angry, but sometimes sorrowful beginning of America's journey to the homestretch; a beginning that started from the singing of the old Negro spiritual *Go Tell it on the Mountain* (which became a famous book title for one of James Baldwin's many lauded publications) to *Amazing Grace.*

Ivor Agyeman-Duah, MSc., MA, (Author),
Centre for Intellectual Renewal, Accra, Ghana

CHRONOLOGY

Photo 1. Malcolm X

Source: By Ed Ford, World Telegram staff photographer - Library of Congress.
New York World-Telegram & Sun Collection. Created: March 12, 1964.
Public Domain, https://commons.wikimedia.org/w/index.php?curid=3515550

1919   It was in this year that the marriage between Baptist Preacher Earl Little of Georgia and Ms. Louise Norton took place. The future mother of Malcolm X was originally from Grenada. At the time known as British West Indies, Americans remember vividly that President Ronald Reagan initiated the invasion of Grenada by U.S. armed forces personnel, a move that contributed to the assassination of the Prime Minister Maurice Rupert Bishop (1944–1983).

1920   The oldest brother of Malcolm X, Wilfred Little, was born in the spring of this year in the state of Pennsylvania.

1923   Itinerant Baptist preacher Earl Little (who was not yet ordained as minister), traveled all over the United States in search of greener pastures as well as preaching opportunities. Finding racial tolerance in Nebraska, he moved with his wife (Mrs. Louise Norton Little) to settle in Omaha, and they were accompanied by their three children.

1925   In this year, Malcolm X is born and named Malcolm Little on May 19 at the local University Hospital in Omaha, Nebraska.

1926   It was in this year that the entire Little family decided, in unison, to settle in Milwaukee, Wisconsin.

1927   After traveling to have consultations with Marcus Garvey, the militant Jamaican nationalist, preacher Earl Little chose to become a leader in his area in Wisconsin for Garvey's United Negro Improvement Association (UNIA). Eventually, Garvey was accused and convicted of mail fraud, jailed, and was later deported from a Georgian jail, where he was serving his sentence. Two years after Malcolm's birth, his younger brother by the name of Reginald is born to the Little family in Milwaukee, Wisconsin.

1928   Earl Little, his wife, and children move to Lansing, Michigan, and they buy a house of their own. Mr. Little's part-time income comes from his work as a preacher for the Baptist church.

1929	In November of this year, the home of the Little family is destroyed by fire that is considered an arson. In December of this year, Earl Little and his wife build a new home in East Lansing, Michigan.
1930	W. D. Fard, considered one of the founders of Nation of Islam (NOI), is honored when his supporters established the first Islamic temple in Detroit, Michigan.
1931	In January, Malcolm is five years-old, and he is enrolled in a kindergarten in the local Pleasant Grove Elementary School. On September 28th, Malcolm's father, Mr. Earl Little, dies from alleged murder that is orchestrated by a KKK-type of supremacist group in town.
1938	Malcolm completes 7th grade in the local West Junior High School, which is based in the Lansing suburb of Michigan.
1939	Given her strange behavior, Mrs. Louise Little is committed to a state mental institution in Kalamazoo, Michigan. For twenty-six years, she remains in the asylum, while Malcolm and other brothers are sent to foster homes. In May of this year, young Malcolm Little starts to work in the position of a handyman for Dr. Gertrude Sullivan. In August, a local social worker recommends that Malcolm should be placed in a home for juveniles. Malcolm begins to study at Mason High School in Mason, Michigan.
1940	Throughout the year, Malcolm is sent to a variety of homes meant for foster children.
1941	In February, Malcolm moves in with his sister, Ella, in Boston MA. Malcolm works as a shoeshine man, a dishwasher, soda jerker, and as a railroad employee. Malcolm involves himself with several shady characters during his stay in Boston.
1942	Malcolm moves to Michigan and works as a porter-messenger.
1943	Malcolm moves to New York and works for the New Haven Railroad and also as a waiter, bartender, a dancer,

and for local restaurants. The U.S. army finds Malcolm unfit for military service.

1944   Malcolm returns to Boston and works for Sears and Roebuck, Co. In November, Malcolm is indicted for larceny and given a three-month suspended sentence. He is placed on probation for one year.

1945   Malcolm moves back to New York. He works as a dancer. In December, Malcolm and his friends go to Boston and engage in series of burglaries.

1946   In January, Malcolm is arrested when he attempts to reclaim a stolen watch that he left for repair at a Boston jewelry store. He is indicted for firearms, larceny, and breaking and entering. In February, Malcolm begins serving his 8–10 year sentence at Charlestown, Massachusetts.

1948   While in prison, Malcolm's younger brother Reginald introduces Malcolm to the teachings of the Honorable Elijah Muhammad. In March, he is transferred to Norfolk Prison Colony in Massachusetts, which provides him with excellent access to books and other reading material.

1952   In August, Malcolm is paroled from the Massachusetts State Prison and he travels to Detroit to live with his brother Wilfred E. Little. While in Detroit, he works as a furniture salesman.

1953   Malcolm works on the assembly line at Ford Motor Company and attends Nation of Islam (NOI) meetings. Malcolm moves to Chicago to study for the ministry and live with Elijah Muhammad. He later serves as the assistant minister of Detroit Temple No. 1. In September, Malcolm becomes the first minister of Boston Temple No.1.

1954   Malcolm serves as a minister and speaker at various Muslim temples. In June, he becomes the minister of New York Temple No. 7.

1955   Malcolm hears rumors that Muhammad is an adulterer.

1956	Betty Sanders joins New York Temple No. 7 and is renamed Betty X.
1957	Hinton Johnson, a member of NOI, is beaten by police and jailed. Malcolm gathers a contingent of Muslims from Temple No. 7 in New York in front of the police station and demands that Johnson be taken to the hospital.
1958	On January 14, Malcolm marries Betty X. They live in an apartment in East Elmhurst, Queens. In November, Malcolm and Betty's first child, Attallah, is born.
1959	Television documentary, "The Hate that Hate Produced," is aired. Malcolm travels to United Arab Republic, Sudan, Nigeria, Egypt, Mecca, Iran, Syria, and Ghana as Muhammad's ambassador.
1960	Malcolm debates with William M. James on WMCA radio regarding the topic: "Is Black Supremacy the Answer." In December, Malcolm and Betty's second daughter, Qubilah, is born.
1961	Malcolm speaks at Harvard Law School forum and debates Walter Carrington of the NAACP. Malcolm leads a protest of Muslims in front of the United Nations to protest the death of prime minister Patrice Lumumba of the Congo.
1962	Malcolm engages in several speeches on college campuses and in Chicago, New York, and Los Angeles regarding racial discrimination and oppression and the futility of integration strategies. In July, Malcolm and Betty's third daughter, Ilyasah, is born. Malcolm X continues to deliver speeches about racial oppression and police violence. Malcolm X speaks with Muhammad's three former secretaries, all of whom have children for him. Malcolm learns that NOI members are leaving the Chicago mosque because of Muhammad's adultery. Malcolm senses strains between his family and Muhammad's family. Muhammad's son Herbert directs editor of the NOI magazine "Muhammad Speaks" to minimize Malcolm's coverage in the magazine.

1963   In May, the New York Times reports Malcolm's criticism
            of President Kennedy for his handling of the Birmingham
            crises. In May, the Amsterdam News reports Malcolm
            attacks the work of Martin Luther King, Jackie Robinson,
            and Floyd Patterson for racial integration. Malcolm
            continues to speak in cities around the country. He attends
            the march on Washington as a critical observer. On
            November 22, President John F. Kennedy is assassinated.
            In December, Malcolm gives his now infamous "Chickens
            Coming Home to Roost" speech. Three days after giving
            the speech, Malcolm is silenced by Muhammad because
            Malcolm disobeyed Muhammad's orders that no minister
            should make any comments about President Kennedy's
            death. Malcolm establishes the Organization of Afro-
            American Unity and Muslim Mosque, Inc.

1964   Malcolm's relationship with Muhammad is strained
            because of Muhammad's silencing of Malcolm and also
            because of rumors that Muhammad has forbidden other
            Muslims from communicating with Malcolm. One of
            Malcolm's former assistants from Mosque No. 7 in New
            York informs Malcolm that the NOI has asked him to wire
            his car with a bomb. Malcolm has an impromptu meeting
            with Martin Luther King as they observe the Senate fili-
            buster over the Civil Rights Bill. In March, the New York
            Times publishes an article discussing the split between
            Muhammad and Malcolm speculating about Malcolm's
            plans to create a new organization. NOI requests that
            Malcolm return all NOI property, including house and car
            to the NOI. Malcolm broadens conflict between himself
            and NOI by airing the dispute in a press conference.
            Malcolm continues to speak in cities and on radio shows
            around the country. In March, Malcolm meets Martin
            Luther King for a face-to-face meeting.

1965   Malcolm speaks to SNCC students who visit Harlem;
            speaks at OAAU rallies, and radio shows in New York
            and New Hampshire and television shows in Canada.
            Malcolm travels to Selma where SNCC is mobilizing

voting rights and speaks at Brown's Chapel AME Church. Malcolm travels to London and attempts to travel to Paris, but he is denied entrance by the French government. In February, Malcolm's house is firebombed. Later that month, his family is evicted from the home. In a conversation with Alex Haley, Malcolm X expresses concerns that the violent threats and incidents may be instigated by people other than the Muslims. On February 21, Malcolm X is assassinated at an OAAU Rally at the Audubon Ballroom. He is pronounced dead on arrival at Columbia Presbyterian Hospital. Martin Luther King sends a telegram to Betty Shabazz to express his sadness and grief over Malcolm's death. Norman 3X Butler is arrested for Malcolm's murder. On February 27, Malcolm is funeralized at Faith Temple Church of God in Christ in New York. Ossie Davis gives the eulogy. Malcolm is buried at Ferncliff Cemetary in Hartsdale, New York. The Autobiography of Malcolm X, written in collaboration with Alex Haley (famous author of *Roots*), is published. Betty Shabazz delivers twin daughters, Malaak and Malikah.

1966   Malcolm's murder trial begins.

1975   Elijah Muhammad dies.

1978   A close associate of the Honorable Elijah Muhammad, Louis Farrakhan, takes over as leader of the NOI.

1995   In January, the FBI accused Malcolm's daughter Quibilah to conspiring to kill Louis Farrakhan, who the family holds responsible for creating the environment that led to Malcolm's assassination. In May, the charges against Quibilah, Malcolm X's daughter, were dropped if she agreed to undergo treatment for chemical dependency and avoid any other crimes.

1997   Betty Shabazz dies in a fire accident that is allegedly triggered by her then twelve-year-old grandson, Malcolm, named for her husband Malcolm X. Malcolm, the son of Qubilah, allegedly caused the fire incident because he wanted to create an incident that would prompt the grandmother to let him leave the house to go and live with his mother, who was one charged with threatening Louis Farrakhan's life.

2010   Article about Malcolm X's killer indicates that other suspected killers were never apprehended.

2011   Columbia University late professor Manning Marable's new book on Malcolm X, with the title of *A Life of Reinvention: Malcolm X*, prompts Malcolm's friends and admirers to publish a book critical of Dr. Manning's 594-page book.

2013   Grandson Malcolm is killed in an unfortunate Mexico City night club incident. The family of Malcolm X subsequently issued a statement to acknowledge the death of the young Malcolm, whose death reminded the family of earlier deaths of his great grandfather (Mr. Earl Little) and his grandfather (Malcolm X).

Malcolm's Travels, 1964–1965

In April, Malcolm travels to Germany, Mecca, Saudi Arabia, Beirut, Cairo, Nigeria, Ghana, Liberia, Senegal, and Morocco. While in Mecca, he performs the Islamic Haj to acquire the Hajj (or Alhaji) title.

In May, Malcolm returns to New York and continues to debate and give speeches around the country.

At the end of May, his Muslim Mosque sponsors a forum at the Audubon Ballroom in New York. Malcolm indicates that his split with Muhammad involved Muhammad's adultery and fathering of six illegitimate children.

In June, Malcolm calls the Civil Rights Bill a farce and discusses the Organization of Afro-American Unity (OAAU), a group that he has organized to do "whatever necessary to bring the Negro struggle from the level of civil rights to the level of human rights."

New York Post publishes open letter from Malcolm to Muhammad calling for an end to the hostilities between them.

Malcolm reports several acts of attempted violence and threats on his life to New York police officers.

Acting on the eviction notice filed by the NOI, a New York judge orders Malcolm and his family to vacate the East Elmhurst property by January 31, 1965.

Malcolm travels abroad to Cairo. He attends the African Summit Conference as a representative of the OAAU. He asks the delegates of the African nations to bring the cause of twenty-two million black people in the U.S. before the U.N. He visits with heads of states in several African countries, including Kenya, Uganda, Tanzania, and Conakry (Guinea).

In November, Malcolm speaks in Paris and returns to New York.

Malcolm travels to Oxford, England where he debates at one of the colleges at Oxford University.

In December, Malcolm returns to the United States and gives speeches at Harvard and in Harlem.

In December, Louis Walcott, who later becomes Louis Farrakhan, writes an article in "Muhammad Speaks" newspaper that Malcolm is worthy of death, words that Mr. Farrakhan has regretted in recent years as a black Muslim leader. In December, Malcolm and Betty's fourth daughter, Amiliah, is born.

CHAPTER 1

MALCOLM X'S NORTH AFRICAN INTERLUDE

BEGINNING OF HIS AFRICAN CONNECTIONS

Many Africans, who saw Malcolm X dressed in African clothes, described the former Nation of Islam (NOI) spokesman and confidante of the late Honorable Elijah Muhammad as being handsomely dressed. They also saw him as a true Pan-Africanist. That was after his second substantive 1964 journey to Africa as non-member of Elijah Muhammad's NOI, and less than a year before his untimely death when he was assassinated in the Audubon Ballroom in Harlem, New York.

MALCOLM X: THE BEGINNING OF HIS AWARENESS OF AFRICAN ISSUES SINCE 1957

In 1957 Malcolm X did not necessarily have the cultural and educational awareness that would draw him closer to Africa. That was why he made a disparaging comment in the fall of 1957 after an African cabinet member of a newly declared independent nation had fallen victim to America's then reigning vicious, racial conditions. It was in Dover, Delaware when

Ghana's finance minister (or finance secretary) was taken for an African American and, therefore, shabbily treated at a restaurant.

Sharply dressed in Western-style suit and tie, Mr. Komla Agbeli Gbedemah (who was famously known by his first two initials, as K.A. Gbedemah) looked very much like any black American. Therefore, when he walked into a Dover restaurant, "he was mistaken for an African-American" (DeCaro 1996, 124). As a result, the restaurant's employees, who traditionally made it a point of not serving blacks who walked in boldly from the front door also refused to serve him like everybody else. Mr. Gbedemah and the Ghana Embassy in Washington, D.C. quickly lodged an official complaint with the U.S. Department of State.

At the time, Ghana diplomatically occupied a special importance after its independence on March 6, 1957, when its name was changed from that of the Gold Coast to that of the ancient African empire (Ghana). The complaint that was lodged was taken seriously, and its consequences were felt far and near, causing U.S. President Dwight "Ike" Eisenhower and his vice president, Mr. Richard M. Nixon, to huddle together to find a solution. Since Nixon led the official U.S. delegation to Ghana's independence festivities, it was felt that he would have a cordial relationship with Mr. Gbedemah, a very significant nationalist politician, who worked very hard when his party's leader, the late President Kwame Nkrumah, was in British colonial prison back in the former Gold Coast due to his agitation for Ghanaian independence.

President Eisenhower decided personally to face the embarrassing issue head on. Therefore, he invited Mr. Gbedemah to the White House the next morning for breakfast, an invitation that the Ghanaian finance minister accepted with gratitude. Those familiar with the issue underscored later that President Eisenhower told Mr. Gbedemah to eat and have as much drink as he wished, especially since his stop at the Dover restaurant was supposedly to get something to drink. At the time, Malcolm X, as an important black Muslim leader with the title of the National Spokesperson of the NOI, was in Detroit, Michigan to address an Islamic group, during which he read in the local newspapers of the Gbedemah incident as well as the reaction of President Eisenhower to the whole scenario. He, who had changed his original name of Malcolm Little to his current name (as Malcolm X), was not in the least amused by the incident. So he seized the chance to inform his Detroit Islamic audience of his displeasure and also that, in his opinion, a black person from outside of the United States was not to be mistreated like local black people, who had slave names and lived in America (Assensoh and Alex-Assensoh 2014).

Malcolm X did not come out either flatly or categorically to raise an objection to the seemingly nice way the Eisenhower White House resolved the embarrassing incident created by the Dover restaurant involving Ghana's then Finance Minister Gbedemah. The American government, through its embassy in the Ghanaian capital of Accra, knew that Mr. Gbedemah was a key member of the Nkrumah government, which was ushered into power barely a year previously in March 1957. Therefore, it would have been suicidal in international relations for American officials to close their eyes to what happened to such an international diplomat, although Malcolm X and possibly other NOI leaders did not see it that way at the time. For example, it was a fact that Nkrumah and Gbedemah planned the strategy for the Convention People's Party (CPP) in the very general elections that were won by Nkrumah's group for the handover of political power by the British. In the elections, Nkrumah agreed to stand for a position in the legislative assembly in the Accra Central Constituency, within the country's capital area, while Mr. Gbedemah went to the Volta Region of the country to contest the elections in Keta area, a strategy that proved successful (Nkrumah 1957).

It was also at the time that Malcolm X was simply looking at Muslims as having an international pull, whereby his own NOI could have an international affiliation with what he saw as the dark-Muslim world, which would involve Muslims in Asia and Africa. In his opinion, with such international connections, the American leaders, by reason of what he saw as of an embarrassment or fear, might deem it necessary to agree to practice what he considered to be racial justice. Author Louis A. DeCaro, Jr. offered a further clarification. He, as a result, pointed out in his book, *On the Side of My People: A Religious Life of Malcolm X*, that there was an irony in the fact that for Malcolm to reach out toward the so-called dark world in general and its Islamic faith, Malcolm X was basically initiating what was deemed to be an evolution of his own religious as well as political understanding (DeCaro 1996).

In the foregoing contexts, Malcolm X was essentially exposing himself to what was seen as a realization that was to force him, as an Islamic leader, to attempt to bring the entire NOI movement and its leadership along with him in such a direction. Instead, he saw how cultic the NOI and its leadership, led by the Honorable Elijah Muhammad, were. For example, it was widely known that Muhammad and W.D. Fard were, indeed, the founding leaders of the Nation of Islam, but Malcolm would realize in later years that, in the larger Islamic world, including Mecca where he would later go to perform his hajj or pilgrimage, nobody was aware of these NOI leaders, including Mr. Fard, one of the founding NOI leaders (DeCaro 1996).

Although Malcolm X was yet to visit the African continent to meet and interact with its Pan-Africanist leaders as well as the people, he still knew a lot about the continent from the tradition of Caribbean-born Marcus Garvey's Universal Negro Improvement Association (UNIA), to which the black separatist trend in the ideology of Muslims could be traced. Besides, Malcolm X's late Baptist-preacher father (Mr. Earl Little) belonged to and worked collaboratively with the UNIA. Additionally, it was also a historical fact that several Islamic ideas, ideology, and programs have had their origins in the nineteenth century from the UNIA (Clegg 1997).

EARLY AFRICAN INFLUENCES AND FIRST AFRICAN TRIP

It was not surprising that Malcolm X would choose to travel to Egypt on his maiden journey to Africa. First, it was a fact that Malcolm knew from his extensive readings that Egypt was often described as the cradle of civilization. He also followed the bold role Egyptian leaders played in the 1956 Suez Canal crisis, as he had learned that in July 1956 Egyptian leaders, led by President Gamal Abdel Nasser, had stubbornly nationalized the Suez Canal to the annoyance of neighboring nations, including Israel, which promptly invaded Egypt. The British government, which was far away from Egypt, followed suit with a threat to invade Egypt to stop the continuing nationalization of the canal, which opponents of Egypt regarded as an international waterway.

Israel, for example, waited for almost four months, until October 1956, to implement their own invasion, when the Jewish nation realized the displeasure and discomfort the Suez crisis had caused back home. Although American leaders, for political reasons, often supported any Israeli governmental action, the government of President Eisenhower opposed the invasion of Egypt to reverse the nationalization of the canal. Consequently, both Israel and Britain ended their respective invasions (Marable 2011).

Obviously, Malcolm X was reading the local as well as the international newspapers and was, therefore, very much aware of what was going on in Egypt. The positive impressions gleaned from these newspaper reports drew admiration for President Nasser, so the planned visit to Egypt seemed very special for Malcolm X. In fact, he preached an entire Islamic sermon on the Egyptian crisis, whereby he subsequently ended it by saying gleefully that black men had united in Egypt to fight whites, whom he referred to at the time—just as his boss, the Honorable Elijah Muhammad did—as "the devils" (Marable 2011).

Malcolm was also aware of the fact that President Nasser and several other African leaders, including the then Ghanaian president Kwame Nkrumah, were actively involved in the Afro-Asian Solidarity Conference (AASC) that had been planned for Bandung, Indonesia, and which was being vigorously promoted by Indonesian President Sukarno. It was the non-aligned movement's conference, to which like-minded leaders of developing countries—sometimes referred to as Third World nations—came together to engage in dialogue on issues, which included being independent of (non-aligned to) the ideological-*cum*-political blocs of the East and West, which strove to outmaneuver each other through Cold War rhetoric. Irrespective of Malcolm X's efforts to rely on published information to get acquainted with Africa, the second largest continent in the world, he realized that he needed to be familiar with African political and diplomatic leaders, who could provide him with reliable information about their respective countries.

As NOI's spokesperson nationally, Malcolm's travels to various regions of the United States, including New York from where he originated, provided him with much-needed contacts. At the United Nations head-quarters in New York City, for example, newly independent African nations had appointed brilliant but brand new, radical ambassadors as permanent representatives (or ambassador extraordinary emissaries), some of whom would prove very useful to Malcolm X in his quest for allies from the motherland, and also as he was planning to travel to Africa for the first time in 1959. The top African diplomats at the United Nations, whose well-educated backgrounds fascinated Malcolm X, included Ghana's United Nations ambassador Alex Quaison-Sackey and Guinean United Nations ambassador Boubacar Diallo Telli, a fellow Muslim, who later on also served as Guinea's ambassador to the United States of America. As fate would have it, both Quaison-Sackey and Telli arrived at the U.N. headquarters at about the same time. Both men had distinguished Western education and, later, civil-service training. Since Malcolm X had very formidable relationships with the two diplo-mats, a brief biographical information about both of them is in order to educate readers about these prominent individuals, whose credentials are supposed to have impressed Malcolm X.

Malcolm X's Friends at the United Nations Headquarters in New York

French-educated Telli was a Guinean diplomat and political figure, with training in law and diplomacy, having earned his law degree (*License en Droit*) in 1951 as well as his doctorate in law in 1954 from the Ecole Nationale de la France d'Outre-Mer in Paris. Before coming to the United Nations, as Guinea's top diplomat, he served in the French West African administrative services, including appointments in the former Dahomey (now called the Republic of Benin) and Senegal, serving as a district attorney (*procereur*) in Senegal. He later became the high commissioner of French West Africa followed by a stint of almost two years as secretary-general in the colonial service, with his residence in Dakar, Senegal.

After Guinea's "*non*" vote in the September 28, 1958, referendum to decide as whether or not the country should attain independence within the French community, headed by France's president Charles de Gaulle, newly elected president Sekou Toure sent Telli to the United Nations in 1958 as Guinea's permanent representative until June 1964. The only pause in his UN duties occurred between April 1959 and June 1961 when Telli served as Guinea's U.S. ambassador, and during which time he and Malcolm X would meet and become close friends.

When the erstwhile Organization of African unity (OAU) was established in 1963 after marathon meetings of African heads of state, Diallo Telli became its first secretary-general at the organization's headquarters in Addis Ababa, Ethiopia. He held this position for two consecutive four-year terms, from July 1964 to June 1972. Diallo Telli also served his country of Guinea as its justice minister (secretary) from August 1972 to July 1976. A year later (in 1977), Telli reportedly died in a Sekou Toure political prison at Camp Boiro, allegedly for being labelled a spy for a Western agency.

While his Guinean counterpart received his higher education from France, Ghana's UN ambassador Quaison-Sackey earned his degrees from Exeter College, University of Oxford, a Lincoln's Inn law studies and a postgraduate diploma in international relations from London School of Economics (Jenkins and Tryman 2002, 454). After Ghana's independence in March 1957, the newly named Prime Minister Nkrumah appointed Quaison-Sackey to the UN position in 1959, and he served there as Ghana's permanent representative until 1965. Ambassador Quaison-Sackey acquitted himself creditably in this assignment. For this reason he was elected to serve as the president of the United Nations General Assembly, the first black person to be placed in that viable capacity (Jenkins and Tryman 2002, 454). When Quaison-Sackey left his United Nations ambassadorial position, he returned to Ghana to serve initially as the country's foreign minister until February 24, 1966, when the Nkrumah regime was overthrown in a military-*cum*-police *coup d'etat*.

Mississippi State University (MSU) history professor Richard V. Damms provided very crucial and credible information about Malcolm and the Ghanaian diplomat in some of his published writings, including a chapter that he contributed to *The Malcolm X Encyclopedia,* published in 2002 by Greenwood Press and co-edited by MSU history professor Robert L. Jenkins and the late MSU political science professor Mfanya Donald Tryman. Malcolm was very fascinated by Dr. Quaison-Sackey's impeccable anti-colonialist credentials. According to Damms, the Ghanaian diplomat was known to be "a fiery opponent of colonialism, racism and apartheid and a staunch Pan-Africanist" (Jenkins and Tryman 2002).

Professor Damms added that Dr. Quaison-Sackey did develop a personal friendship with Malcolm X, and that just as the black Muslim leader felt, the Ghanaian diplomat "viewed the African American struggle in the United States as part of a larger African struggle" (Jenkins and Tryman 2002, 455). Although Dr. Quaison-Sackey had to be very diplomatic in his utterances about American racial matters, he still found a way to team up with Malcolm X and other diplomats in condemning what they saw as American intervention in Third World revolutionary activities, particularly in 1960s. They were alarmed by the political unrest going on in the Congo (later Congo-Kinshasa), headed at the time by elected prime minister Patrice Lumumba. As stated earlier, the Congo is today known as the Democratic Republic of the Congo (DRC). The Ghanaian diplomat (Quaison-Sackey), who developed a personal friendship with Malcolm X, utilized his position as the president of the United Nations General Assembly to assist Malcolm X in mobilizing UN opposition to what Malcolm considered to be U.S. violations of African American human rights (Jenkins and Tryman 2002, 455).

Another influential African who crossed paths with Malcolm X and would make a strong recommendation for a visit to Africa by Malcolm was a Nigerian scholar, Dr. E.U. Essien-Udom, who researched and wrote one of the first-hand accounts of the Nation of Islam (NOI) as well as black nationalism in general. His 1962 book, *Black Nationalism: A Search for an Identity in America*, was written from information and research that brought him in contact with Malcolm X and the NOI leader, Muhammad. Before completing his publication, Dr. Essien-Udom had been a graduate student in the mid-1950s at the University of Chicago. When attending NOI meetings to gather information for his book, the Nigerian scholar met and talked with Malcolm X. Essien-Udom is one of those who wrote that toward the end of his life, Malcolm X expanded and internationalized the struggle for his own independence including seeking to link his fellow blacks with African liberation struggles. Above all, Dr. Essien-Udom was quoted as having focused on Malcolm X's transformation from the national spokesperson for the NOI "to an international spokesman for the people in the Third World, in which Malcolm used the phrase *black revolution* in this context" (Jenkins and Tryman 2002, 206–207). Malcolm got to know Dr. Essien-Udom well, an explanation for why he would play host to Malcolm X in Nigeria despite not being a Muslim. Still, someone like Guinea's UN Ambassador Telli, a Muslim, had a lot of influence on Malcolm X; yet, Nigerian professor E. Essien-Udom and Ghana's Ambassador Quaison-Sackey, although not Muslims, also still had a lot of influence on Malcolm X and they were close to him, as further discussed in the concluding part of this book, where Malcolm's legacy is considered.

As a fellow Muslim, Telli was known to have paid great attention to Malcolm X and was also very helpful, in a variety of ways. Malcolm X in turn invited Telli to Islamic mosques for prayer services and to address NOI gatherings. It was on the advice of Telli and other African Muslims that in 1959 Malcolm X agreed to serve as an emissary of the Honorable Elijah Muhammad by travelling to Africa with stopovers mainly in predominantly Muslim countries. The interesting fact was that, at this time, Malcolm and his mentor (Elijah Muhammad), as biographer Claude Andrew Clegg III disclosed in 1997, were not very conversant with the plight of blacks in the Middle East, an important region that Malcolm would visit on his first overseas trip. For example, the NOI leader (Muhammad) was supposed to be only vaguely aware of stories about slavery in the Islamic or Arab world. Professor Clegg went on to divulge that Saudi Arabia, which he described as being the cradle of Islam and has the two important pilgrimage places of Medina and Mecca, did not "officially emancipate its one hundred thousand plus African bondmen until November 1962" (Clegg 1997, 122).

Interestingly, Muhammad glossed over details of black suffering in the Islamic world, and he did everything possible and within his power to create the impression that blacks in America and Muslims everywhere were largely kin, adding to the fallacy that, indeed, no Muslim will in any way enslave another Muslim. However, if Muhammad was aware of the enslavement of blacks in the Muslim world of the Middle East, then the NOI leader and his followers were hypocritical by overlooking the condemnable actions of one slave master (i.e. the United States and the Western world in general), but adopting names as well as the religious practices of another group of slave masters, as Clegg points out in his biography of the NOI leader. However, in spite of the poignant revelation that there was racial discrimination and enslavement of blacks in the

Islamic world, Muhammad decided, ahead of time, to dispatch his leading lieutenant or valuable mentor in Malcolm X to several places in Africa and the Middle East (Clegg 1998).

As part of the plans for Malcolm X to commence his overseas trip in Egypt, considered by Malcolm and other NOI leaders as the cradle of civilization, several activities had to be embarked upon first. For example, measures were put in place for Arabic speakers to be hired for NOI schools. Also, NOI ministers were, for the first time, encouraged to make qualitative references to the Holy *Qur'an*, which was seen as the Islamic guide book, just as the Holy Bible had always been for Christians for many years. Also, Malcolm learned from his solid United Nations connections that, in 1958, the second non-aligned meeting of the Afro-Asian Solidarity Organization, similar to the Bandung meeting in Indonesia, was taking place in Egypt, with President Nasser as its host. Therefore, in the spirit of what he described as confraternity, Malcolm X encouraged Muhammad, as NOI leader, to cable a message of congratulations and solidarity to Cairo and wish President Nasser and other non-aligned leaders well. According to Marable, the Egyptian leader was deeply touched, so much so that in the following year the Honorable Elijah Muhammad received similar fraternal greetings during the year's Savior's Day observance from Egyptian President Nasser in reciprocation of what was sent during the non-aligned summit in the Egyptian capital (Marable 2011).

As has been documented by several scholars, President Nasser's Egypt was also believed to have much fascination with Malcolm X causing him to place that country at the top of the list of countries he was to visit in 1959. In fact, the main reason for the allure was that he was considered a student of history, who had familiarized himself with Egyptian civilization by reading very widely. Malcolm was known to have taken NOI members and their families to museums, where he reportedly got the tourists to learn a lot about Africa and its rich history. He was known to be highly impressed by the meaningful contribution of black people to Egyptian history in the contexts of African history in general.

Most certainly, the major opportunity came for Malcolm to deepen his preparations to travel to Africa when he was appointed by the Honorable Elijah Muhammad to head the Nation of Islam (NOI) Mosque No.7 in Harlem. It was there that he would also meet his future wife, at the time known as Ms. Betty Sanders, to whom Malcolm X would, on January 12, 1958, make a marriage proposal, which Betty accepted. This proposal was made while standing in a phone booth in Detroit. A year later on January 4, 1959, Malcolm and Betty got married in Lansing. Those at the simple wedding ceremony were his two brothers Wilfred and Philbert, who had strongly encouraged him to become an active member of the NOI (Jenkins and Tryman 2002; Marable 2011).

MALCOLM X'S INITIAL VISIT TO AFRICA

Malcolm X had been married for only seven months when he got ready to travel to Africa and the Middle East. It meant that he was to leave his young wife Betty for this assignment as he was happy to serve the NOI leader in any way, including representing Elijah Muhammad as his emissary abroad. Therefore, around July 4, 1959, Malcolm left the United States for Egypt, which he described to his family members and friends as the land of the pharaohs. The journey to Egypt, in particular, had been well planned for him by Egyptian diplomats and his friends in the African diplomatic corps. He was received officially by Egyptian leaders, including the vice-president Anwar Al-Sadat. Showing deference to the NOI leader Muhammad, Malcolm X declined several opportunities to meet president Gamal Abdel Nasser of Egypt, principally because "he believed that this privilege should be reserved for his teacher, Elijah Muhammad" (Clegg 1997; Jenkins and Tryman 2002).

Illness interrupted part of Malcolm X's visit to Egypt. Without knowing exactly what he ate to incur this malady, Malcolm X suffered from persistent diarrhea, which affected his scheduled trips to various countries other than Egypt. In fact, he had to prolong his stay in Egypt about three days. Consequently, he could only make brief visits to Damascus and

Jerusalem before journeying to Saudi Arabia, where he was only able to visit Jeddah but not Mecca, as he had previously planned to do. Due to ill health, his travel itinerary to several African countries, including Ethiopia, Nigeria, and Ghana, was curtailed. Although he felt that he had learned a lot on the trip and would return to the United States with credible information to contribute useful information to assist Elijah Muhammad in planning his own trip to Africa, it was still a fact that he did not stay long enough on that journey. Malcolm, however, did have an eye-opening outlook on various situations, including learning about the differences between the NOI brand of Islam and the Islam that he encountered in Egypt and other places in the Middle East. To Malcolm X's surprise, he was to learn, during his travels that in several places in the area that he was scheduled to visit, including Saudi Arabia and its Holy cities like Mecca and Medina, "there were tens of thousands of pilgrims from all over the world. They were of all colors, from blue-eyed blonds to black-skinned Africans" (Malcolm X 1999, 346).

Malcolm's transformational experience from his Egyptian trip was the fact that he could now consider himself an international traveler. He also felt particularly well received by Egyptian scholars and students alike when he fulfilled an invitation to lecture at Egypt's Al-Azhar University. Dysentery prolonged Malcolm's stay in Egypt, so he found time to visit several historic sites, including the pyramids. However, he realized that his lack of Arabic language was a handicap, especially when he was expected to visit mosques to pray five times a day as true Muslims did. He did not hide his shortcoming, as he confessed it to some of the Egyptian leaders whom he could confide in, who then wondered about the viability or efficacy of what was being taught by NOI to its members with respect to Islam. It was while in Egypt that Malcolm felt that there was no racial or ethnic tensions in the country, which therefore confirmed for him the absence of prejudices when it came to issues of color, and that all Muslims were equal before Allah or God (Marable 2011).

By spending about three weeks on the trip, Malcolm did learn about the liberation struggles of various African countries to which he was not able to visit due to time. It included Algeria's National Liberation Front (NLF), which was battling France for the country's freedom from colonialism. He also learned a lot about the liberation struggles in West Africa, where U.S.-educated leaders like Nigeria's first president Nnamdi Azikiwe as well as Ghana's Kwame Nkrumah and French-educated Ahmed Sekou Toure of Guinea had led liberation struggles to shake off colonial yokes in their respective countries. While away, Malcolm X found the time to send written correspondence, in the form of letters and postcards, to NOI colleagues, some of which were "filled with new ideas about Islam and Afro-Asian solidarity" (Marable 2011, 167).

Some of Malcolm's letters went to his friends in the U.S. press, and one of them was in fact published in the *Pittsburg Courier*, in which he discussed the fact that many of the Muslims he met on his trip were not necessarily black men and women, but that they were of a different racial or ethnic mix. The 1959 trip was also well publicized in NOI circles and by black newspapers in the United States. Plans were also afoot for the NOI leader to travel, later in the year, to the Middle East and some places in Africa (Marable 2011, 169). Although Malcolm returned to the United States happy that he had, at least, seen part of Africa during his brief trip, he was very careful not to harp on the negative things that he saw when he was travelling. It was much later after he had left the Nation of Islam and formed his own organizations that he was known to have alluded to the type of slavery that Malcolm either saw or suspected. According to Professor Clegg, he was known to have "made a few comments against slavery, no matter who it's carried on by" (Clegg 1997, 124).

Still a member of the NOI, Malcolm returned to the United States toward the end of July 1959 to help plan Muhammad's overseas trip. It was on his arrival in the United States that he was on July 26, 1959, asked to accompany his mentor and teacher (Muhammad) to St. Nicholas Arena, where he was to introduce Muhammad to the audience. Malcolm utilized the opportunity to speak briefly about his recent trip to Africa and some parts of the Middle East. Muhammad received a long standing ovation before he even spoke. He called for unity among American blacks and other blacks, adding that there would be a time when black people in America would return to Africa, describing them as the biblical lost sheep, to a thunderous applause. He invited his son, Wallace Muhammad, head of Philadelphia-based Mosque No. 12, to speak after him. He also called for unity because, in an accusatory tone, he claimed that the white establishment in America sought to divide black people. He also attacked the media, which gave a lot of publicity to the screened video titled "The Hate That Hate Produced," which aired when Malcolm X was out of the country. Later on, Muhammad's three-year regularly published column in *Pittsburgh Courier* was dropped, mainly after *Time Magazine* had described the NOI leader as "purveyor of this cold black hatred" (Clegg, 1998).

Malcom and other NOI ministers were worried that the anti-NOI backlash was taking place while Muhammad was preparing to travel overseas in the fall of 1959. To make matters worse, the Detroit *Free Press* announced on August 15, 1959, that the city had ordered the closure of the University of Islam, which was operated by NOI temple No. 1, and that its 102 students had been asked to relocate elsewhere. During this time, at Rockland Palace in New York, a major event involving over six thousand NOI members was successfully staged by Malcolm X and Wallace Muhammad, which was addressed by the NOI leader.

Malcolm and Wallace spoke bitterly against *Time Magazine* and other publications for their anti-NOI outbursts. To make matters worse, U.S.-based civil rights leaders in Dr. King's camp started their own campaign suggesting that separatist and other inimical NOI teachings were going to undermine efforts to seek full citizenship for American blacks. Executive Secretary Roy Wilkins of the National Association for the Advancement of Colored people (NAACP) issued a statement underscoring the opinion that the NAACP and its leadership "opposes and regards as dangerous any group, white or black, political or religious, that preaches hatred among men" (Clegg 1997, 129).

Meanwhile, other black professionals and religious leaders added their voices to the anti-Muslim campaign. In fact, the most significant of them all was the voice of the Rev. Dr. Martin Luther King, Jr., the civil rights leader. Using an address to the annual meeting in Milwaukee of the predominantly black National Bar Association (NBA), Dr. King openly described the NOI as one of America's "hate groups arising in our midst, which would preach a doctrine of black supremacy" (Clegg 1997, 129–130). Dr. King also went on to urge his followers to toe the path of nonviolence and not to stoop to what he described as low and primitive methods of some of his movement's opponents. An important legal luminary in the person of the director of the Legal Defense and Education Fund of the NAACP, Thurgood Marshall, who eventually became the first black justice of the Supreme Court, described the NOI as possibly being "run by a bunch of thugs organized from prisons and jails, and financed, I am sure, by [Egyptian president] Nasser or some Arab group" (Clegg 1997, 129).

Muhammad saw attacks on the NOI as the very reason why he should travel overseas to reinvigorate his ideas on Islam. Therefore, it was in early November of that year that Muhammad would start his own journey, accompanied by two of his sons, Herbert and Akbar. His plans included making a pilgrimage to Mecca, but that was not possible because his trip did not coincide with the pilgrimage season. Therefore, instead of a *hajj*, which was the full-blown pilgrimage, he was only able to make the minor pilgrimage known among Muslims as *umrah*. This is considered a spiritual journey to the Holy Land and is highly valued by Muslims but not as important as the *hajj*, which Malcolm would accomplish in 1964 to attain the Islamic title of *El-Hajj* (or *Alhaji*) (Marable 2011).

**FIRST OVERSEAS TRIP TO AFRICA AND THE MIDDLE EAST BY
ELIJAH MOHAMMED**

Malcolm, as expected, promptly and adequately briefed Elijah Muhammad
on the expectations from the Middle East and Islamic North Africa.
Therefore, on November 21, 1959, Muhammad and his two sons left the
United States on a flight that would take them to Istanbul, Turkey, after
stopovers in Europe. In the afternoon of November 22nd, the Muhammads
were in Turkey as planned. The NOI leader was fascinated by Turkish
history, including how the capital was moved from Constantinople to
Ankara, which was accomplished in 1923, as Elijah Muhammad was
informed by an Islamic tour guide. For three days, Muhammad and
his two sons visited several places in Turkey, with an emphasis on
Islamic events and centers in the Istanbul area (Clegg 1997, 137). Between
November 25–29, 1959, Muhammad and his sons visited Damascus, Beirut,
and Jerusalem, which was partly controlled by the Kingdom of Jordan.
Muhammad arrived in Cairo on November 29th, the time that Nasser's
Egypt had formed a loose federation with Syria and Yemen, known later
as the United Arab Republic (UAR), with Cairo as its strong center.

Egypt, in the eyes of Muhammad and other Muslims, was a prosperous
place worthy of such a visit, which had been prearranged for a dignified
reception of Elijah Muhammad by Egyptian officials. Both Nasser and
Muhammad were happy to meet each other, during which they discussed
matters that were mutually beneficial to the NOI and the Egyptian leader.
Nasser made sure that Muhammad was given royal treatment, including
visits to pyramids and other Egyptian historic artifacts; Muhammad
learned from Malcolm X how Nasser, aided by Vice-President Sadat,
overthrew King Farouk in 1952 (Clegg 1997).

One place that fascinates blacks in the diaspora is the Sudan, which
often serves as the dividing epoch between North Africa and Sub-Sahara
Africa. Therefore, when Muhammad and his sons left the Egyptian capital
of Cairo, they arrived in Khartoum, the Sudanese capital, on December
16, 1959, with plans to stay there for three days. Upon their arrival,

the Muhammads realized that Sudan was under a military dictatorship because of the *coup d'etat* there in November 1958. The Honorable Elijah Muhammad was used to democratic norms back in America and so was surprised to learn from fellow Muslims that all civil liberties, including freedom of the press, civil, and human rights were not in existence. He also found that just as in several African countries, including oil-rich Nigeria, the economically backward northern region of Sudan was of Arab ancestry and Muslim, while the southern part, populated by black Africans, was predominantly Christian and Africans with traditional beliefs. It was a rude awakening for Muhammad and his children when they further learned that the Islamic majority in Sudan was the most coercive, exhibiting sheer oppression on the rest of the country, similar to what they would see elsewhere.

In fact, through Malcolm X, Muhammad learned a lot about the Ethiopian Empire, which was led at the time by Emperor Haile Selassie, the spiritual head of the Rastafarian group based in the Caribbean. Symbolically, the strong-willed but very intelligent Selassie was dubbed by his people as the "Lion of Judah." Muhammad, who wanted to see African countries as bastions of unity and cohesion, was surprised to learn, upon his arrival in the Ethiopian capital of Addis Ababa, that Ethiopia had its ethnic or tribal cleavages. Elijah Muhammad was greatly aware of the 1936–1941 Italian invasion of Ethiopia (again thanks to Malcolm X's tutorials and the hurried preparation of the NOI leader for his trip), and Muhammad was amazed that Ethiopia had succeeded economically and otherwise despite scanty resources, as Malcolm had rightly pointed out to Muhammad from the knowledge gained through association with African diplomats in the United Nations. Ethiopia was overwhelmingly dominated by the Amharic-speaking citizenry, a stronghold that would prompt the Eritreans, who were still a part of Selassie's Ethiopia, to launch a liberation struggle for independence, which would happen much later. In all, the Muhammads stayed in Africa for a month, but were unprepared to face the many unexpected situations that they confronted. The NOI leader and his children were therefore glad that shortly before

Christmas day in 1959, they were out of Africa bound for Saudi Arabia, arriving at "the port of Jidda [Jeddah] in the coastal Hejaz region of Saudi Arabia" on December 23, 1959 (Clegg 1997, 141).

It was between 1959 and 1960 that both Malcolm X and his mentor (the Honorable Elijah Muhammad) completed their respective maiden visits to Africa and the Middle East. In order to capitalize on their trips to the motherland and the Holy Land of Saudi Arabia, both NOI stalwarts planned to be overtly active in their respective responsibilities. It was, therefore, no surprise that early in the 1960s the Harlem-based Mosque No. 7, headed directly by Malcolm X, deliberately promoted growth in a variety of ways. Malcolm X increased his presence at the United Nations to court African diplomats, particularly those with Islamic credentials. He also took steps to increase activity and to involve the general public in NOI events. For example, with Malcolm's active encouragement, Mosque No. 7 began to organize rallies almost every other week focused on bringing widespread change to what was seen as Harlem's impoverished and embattled black population (Marable 2011).

As a unique strategist, Malcolm X brought home from the trips he and Muhammad embarked upon in Africa and the Middle East the knowledge and experience that could be tapped by the leadership of Mosque No. 7 as well as the general leadership of the NOI. He also extolled the fact that it was auspicious for their mosque to be based in the New York area, where the United Nations was situated, as he already had viable contacts among Third World diplomats that would enhance the status of this institution. At that point, Malcolm felt that since he and Muhammad had paid successful visits to African nations and the Holy Land of Mecca as well as a few other Islamic nations of the Middle East, they had the legitimacy to preach to their respective NOI audiences about the places that they had visited, including comparing notes on Islam as practiced at home and in countries overseas.

Malcolm X and Muhammad worked well until the assassination of U.S. president John F. Kennedy in the fall of 1963. The death of Kennedy affected every segment of American society because of his stature, but Malcolm X was still ready to make insensitive comments about the sad event. For example, after the assassination, Muhammad ordered the NOI leadership not to say anything about it. In fact, he himself decided not to fulfill a December 1, 1963, invitation to speak in order not to be tempted to make any comments about President Kennedy's death. Instead, he asked Malcolm X, his closest lieutenant, to represent him at the scheduled Manhattan center event. In Muhammad's opinion, it was more important for him to utilize the knowledge he had acquired from his overseas trip to improve his NOI operations than to be involved in divisive local politics. For example, with the support of Malcolm X, Muhammad decided to rename his various temples as mosques, which was to be "in line with the designation used throughout the Middle East for places of worship" (Clegg 1997, 141).

Since Muhammad briefly stopped over in Pakistan, before flying to North Africa, he was interested in seeking information on the Ahmadiyya Movement, which he saw as an orthodox Islamic sect that had as its leader Mirza Ghulam Ahmad, considered by his followers to be the nineteenth-century Mahdi. Muhammad saw from what he read that the Pakistani-based movement had teachings that were different from those of his own Nation of Islam. He agreed with the notion that the various doctrines of the Ahmadiyya Movement could be considered to be "ideological precursors of the Muslim movement of Fard Muhammad [the legitimate founder of the NOI]" (Clegg 1997, 143).

Malcolm X was still in a euphoric mood about his trip to the motherland (Africa) and the Holy Land (Mecca). Therefore, he took time to prepare for the lecture on December 1, 1963, making sure that he had provided a topical outline for a lecture that would discuss Islam's spiritual importance including black consciousness, and its effects on black nationalist politics overall. The lecture would also address Pan-Africanism, and the Third World revolution that he foresaw for Africa and the Asiatic nations with interests in the non-aligned nations of the world. Eventually, Malcolm X decided to speak at the December 1st event on "God's Judgment of White America." Apart from extolling Elijah Muhammad as a prophet that could be compared with biblical prophets, Malcolm also endeavored to place the religious practices and beliefs of the Nation of Islam (NOI) in perspective and also "within the larger Muslim world" (Marable 2011, 270).

Malcolm X's speech had been so diplomatically prepared that it avoided any reference to the assassination of President Kennedy until, unfortunately, it came to the question and answer period of the event, when he was tempted to speak about the presidential assassination. Asked for his own opinion about the Kennedy assassination, Malcolm took the opportunity to lambast the Vietnam policies of the Kennedy administration and civil rights issues. He punctuated the outbursts with the following sad comments: "Being an old farm boy myself, chickens coming home to roost never did make me sad; they've always made me glad" (Marable 2011, 272).

Muhammad was incensed, for Malcolm had disobeyed his order that all NOI members should desist from commenting on or saying anything about the Kennedy assassination. Indeed, when Malcolm made his "chickens coming home to roost" comment, Muhammad was not there, but his agents at the event held on December 1, 1963—including one John Ali— had rushed to convey the remarks to the NOI leader. Muhammad invited Malcolm X to the Chicago headquarters of the NOI to explain his defiance of his injunction. Since Malcolm had in the past made more sensitive comments and got away with them, he did not see anything terribly bad about the Kennedy assassination comments that he uttered at the Manhattan center event. In fact, he clearly remembered how he described as a beautiful thing the June 3, 1962, deaths of over one hundred Georgia political and business leaders, in a plane crash, praying that God (or the Islamic Allah) would let more such planes drop from the sky to show His displeasure with white Americans. Indeed, Malcolm did not expect any punishment for making the comments about the Kennedy assassination. His visit to Elijah Muhammad in Chicago coincided with his monthly trips to the windy city but, as far as Muhammad was concerned, he was wrong (Clegg 1998; Malcolm X 1999).

While Muhammad was waiting for the arrival of Malcolm X, he thought about many scenarios, including the need to take steps—even if it meant humiliating Malcolm X—to show who was, indeed, in control of NOI affairs. Muhammad was also a strategist; he knew that if he did anything to drive away Malcolm from the Nation of Islam (NOI), he and his followers could revolt. Were this to happen, the NOI would lose some of its members. Yet, Muhammad felt that he had an auspicious moment to discipline Malcolm X and, if anything, to do so in order "to safeguard himself against any future challenges to his leadership" (Clegg 1997, 204).

Muhammad's plan was to suspend Malcolm for several days, during which time he would do nothing on behalf of the NOI. Therefore, as part of the upcoming punishment, Muhammad asked Captain Joseph X to take charge of Mosque No. 7 on an interim basis. Malcolm had known from an earlier conversation with Muhammad that he was in serious trouble, and that their scheduled post–1964 New Year meeting would not be a pleasant affair. To make sure that Malcolm X knew what was in store for him, Muhammad went ahead to ask Newark mosque-leader minister James Shabazz to become the permanent head of Harlem-based Mosque No. 7. For the suspension announcement, Muhammad invited Malcolm to his Phoenix, Arizona hideout. Elijah Muhammad needed witnesses, so he asked John Ali and Raymond Sharrieff to be present at his January 6, 1964, meeting with Malcolm X. Apart from the Kennedy assassination comment, Muhammad also confronted Malcolm X about information that he was part of the rumors about Muhammad's infidelities, etc. After suspending Malcolm from the NOI for ninety days, he told Malcolm: "Go back and put out the fire you started" (Clegg 1997, 207).

PARTING FROM NOI AND SUBSEQUENT TRIPS TO AFRICA AND THE MIDDLE EAST

Not pleased with what he saw as his humiliation by Elijah Muhammad, Malcolm X decided to leave the Nation of Islam (NOI). That was to sadden many NOI and non-NOI members because Malcolm X and Elijah Muhammad were so close that the NOI leader "took the news of Malcolm's departure [from the Nation] hard" (Clegg 1997, 213). However, their relationship became strained following the suspension (Jenkins and Tryman 2002, 361). The ninety-day suspension had prompted the imminent termination of the long-existing special and cordial relationship between Malcolm X and his teacher-*cum*-mentor Muhammad. Since Elijah Muhammad did not make any effort to lift the suspension, as expected, Malcolm felt that the NOI leader simply did not want him back. Consequently, on March 8, 1964, Malcolm announced his departure from the NOI in order to start his own movement, although he made it clear in his public announcement that he would remain a Muslim. He also explained that for Islamic matters and propagation of its teachings, he was establishing the Muslim Mosque, Inc. (MMI) as well as a more political organization that he named the Organization of Afro-American Unity (OAAU), both of which would be based in the New York area (Jenkins and Tryman 2002, 361–362).

At the New York Park Sheraton Hotel press conference establishing the MMI, for example, Malcolm X disclosed his new philosophy, which included the fact that the MMI would provide a religious base for handling issues and problems affecting America's black communities. The OAAU would also have a political program that would be based on what he saw as black nationalism. For the OAAU, he established a black brain trust to work on the publication of a six-page document of aims and objectives. Malcolm was so serious about his new organizations that on March 16, 1964, he filed a certificate of incorporation in the New York area, locating its headquarters in Hotel Theresa, where he once met then Cuban leader Fidel Castro (Marable 2011; Jenkins and Tryman 2002).

By coincidence, about three weeks after Malcolm left the NOI, he was for the first time to meet face-to-face, on March 26, 1964, with the Reverend Dr. Martin Luther King, Jr. in the U.S. Capitol during the discussion of several aspects of the 1964 Civil Rights Act. Both men shook hands warmly. Following that meeting, Malcolm started to distant himself from his past anti-white rhetoric, including refining his bitter "The Ballot or the Bullet" speech, which was re-delivered at an April 3, 1964, public lecture at the Cory Methodist Church in Cleveland—an event that was hosted by the Cleveland branch of the Congress of Racial Equality (CORE). In fact, he used the lecture to sue for black unity. The Federal Bureau of Investigation (FBI), which monitored the lecture event, saw the modification in the speech, which was in fact appealing to blacks and whites alike. While these events were taking place, Malcolm was planning another trip to Africa for the middle of April 1964. Before he could begin the trip, his former Mosque No. 7 leaders instituted a court action aimed at evicting Malcolm and his family from the Queens home in which they lived. New York attorney Percy Sutton was retained by Malcolm X to fight the suit, at least to buy time to make sure that Betty and his children would not be thrown out of their home (Marable 2011).

Around April 13, 1964, Malcolm flew from New York to Cairo, where he was welcomed by old friends, including African leaders who were attending that year's annual meeting of the Organization of African Unity (OAU), which is today called the African Union (AU). He learned that he could accompany some Muslim friends he had made to Jeddah to perform the *hajj* pilgrimage. After solving some immigration problems and establishing his Islamic credentials, Malcolm was happy that at long last, he was to undertake the *hajj*, which would mark him as a mainstream Muslim. He did as all pilgrims did, including circling the *Kaaba* and accompanying other pilgrims to Mina to perform other essential pilgrimage activities. From the pilgrimage, Malcolm flew to Beirut, where he stayed at the local Palm Beach Hotel, from where he visited the campus of the American University in the Lebanese capital.

After his pilgrimage, he decided to travel to other countries of the Middle East.

Malcolm X was aware of the Algerian struggle for independence from some of the young indigenous Algerians, who were seen as anti-French colonial leaders. He was saddened by some of the stories he heard, including how, in 1962, the French officials had engaged in what Malcolm X was informed to be bloodletting in Algeria, which eventually led to the independence of the African country that year. Determined to see things for himself, Malcolm X added to his plans a trip to Algeria in 1964. After his brief stopover in Paris, where he chose to stay at Hotel Terminus St. Lazare, he flew to the Algerian capital of Algiers in November 1964. Just as in Dakar, the Senegalese capital, Malcolm X had a rude re-awakening for he had to reckon with the French language, which served as the official language of these places. As a result, he could not have a successful visit in the French-speaking country, for it dawned on him that he could neither speak nor understand the colonial language, French. Apart from visiting some tourist places in the capital, Malcolm decided to leave Senegal.

CHAPTER 2

MALCOLM X'S JOURNEYS TO WEST AFRICA

Although Malcolm X had plans to visit West African nations and some of its leaders in May 1964, he still decided to pass through Egypt, his second visit to the area. He had planned his 1964 visit to Africa in such a way that, by July 1964, he would be in the Egyptian capital of Cairo in order to serve as an observer of that year's meeting of heads of state of the Organization of African Unity (OAU).

However, in early May, Malcolm arrived in Nigeria, where he stayed at the Federal Palace Hotel, from where his good friend, professor E.U. Essien-Udom picked him up and took him on a tour of Lagos, then the capital of Nigeria (Marable 2011, 313–314). Malcolm had an exciting trip to Nigeria, where he received royal and traditional treatment (including a Yoruba name), but he wrote later in his diary and also said in press interviews that during his April–May 1964 overseas trip, he regarded the Ghana portion of the trip as the highlight. Apart from meeting several voluntarily exiled African American men and women—including Mrs. Shirley Graham DuBois—Malcolm X was also happy that he had the chance to meet and hold discussions with Ghana's president Kwame

Nkrumah, the foremost Pan-Africanist. Just as he did at the University of Ibadan, Malcolm also gave a successful lecture at the University of Ghana. Malcolm X, who later visited East African nations including Kenya and Tanzania, made it abundantly clear that through Ghana's then UN Ambassador Quaison-Sackey and Guinean Ambassador Telli, he had learned a lot about Africa's decolonization struggles as well as how the late presidents Kwame Nkrumah and Sekou Toure of Ghana and Guinea, respectively, welcomed diaspora-based blacks with open arms. Nkrumah rolled out the red carpet for African Americans like St. Claire Drake, Leslie Lacy, and others to whom the new indigenous leader of the then Gold Coast launched his initial "appeal for technical aid and recruitment for the Gold Coast, and they in turn promised to give every assistance by way of publicity and propaganda" (Nkrumah 1957, 164).

According to Ambassador Quaison-Sackey, Malcolm X was supposed to have received a copy of Dr. Nkrumah's June 1951 commencement address at Lincoln University in Pennsylvania, during which he, as titular political leader of the British colony of the Gold Coast (now called Ghana), received the honorary Doctor of Laws (LL.D.) from president Horace Mann Bond, the father of NAACP chairman emeritus Julian Bond. The leader of government business, the position Nkrumah had assumed in the colonial administration, was deeply touched by this honor, for this had occurred not long after he left America, as he said in his own words, "It was just over six years since I had left America, and I could not believe that such an honor could be bestowed upon me in so short a space of time" (Nkrumah 1957, 157).

According to the correspondence which Malcolm X exchanged with several African leaders, including the UN-based diplomats, he was thrilled by the radical anti-colonialist and anti-imperialist statements of Nkrumah and other emerging, indigenous leaders in Africa. For example, in 1951 the Gold Coast leader, who was to lead the colony to independence and then change the country's name to Ghana, gave the commencement address to the Lincoln University faculty, administrators, and students.

In it, Nkrumah spoke about his hopes for the country that he would lead in West Africa in 1957, as the specific date of March 6 for independence, had been tentatively set by the colonial leaders, including the British governor, marking the historic Bond of 1844, the formal arrangement that placed the then Gold Coast colony under formal British control on March 6 of that year. Apart from the speech reiterating the democratic principles that Nkrumah and his political allies planned to introduce, he warned the colonial leaders: "What we want [in the Gold Coast] is the right to govern ourselves, or even to misgovern ourselves" (Nkrumah 1957, 164). Indeed, blacks in America keenly followed Ghana's preparations for independence, as Professor Clegg explained: "the independence of Ghana in 1957 had much to do with [Elijah] Muhammad's renewed emphasis on emigration [to Africa]" (Clegg 1997, 121).

Toward the end of Nkrumah's 1951 commencement address, in which he issued his clarion-call invitation to diaspora-based black men and women, Nkrumah specifically spoke about the needs of the then Gold Coast for technicians as well as machinery and capital for the development of its great natural resources; he further explained that he was appealing to the democracies of Britain and the United States for the much-needed assistance in the first place, but if this request was spurned, Nkrumah would go elsewhere for it, a possible reference to the socialist countries in the midst of the East-West Cold War. In the Lincoln University commencement address, the future president of Ghana went on to speak directly to African Americans, then known as Negroes: "I said that there was much for the Negro people of America to do to help their ancestral country both then and in the future and that, upon attainment of independence, it was the intention of my Party to re-name the country Ghana" (Nkrumah 1957, 164; Assensoh 1998, 97).

The aforementioned calls on diaspora-based blacks and Western nations to come to the assistance of the Gold Coast, poised to become independent with the new name of Ghana yet remain within the British Commonwealth of Nations, created much excitement. The future Ghanaian president Kwame Nkrumah disclosed at a subsequent press conference in New York City, after arriving from the Lincoln University commencement ceremony, that many blacks—including newly graduated men and women—had spoken with him and expressed the desire to travel to the Gold Coast to offer their assistance. At that press conference, President Nkrumah pointed out that his commencement address at his *alma mater* did arouse great interest in his country and, as a result, he was bombarded with a lot of questions about the level of assistance, including the dollar amount, that the Gold Coast needed for development purposes. In addition, some serious-minded and interested blacks also wanted to know the "conditions of service for interested technicians and other pertinent matters arising from my address" (Nkrumah 1957, 164).

The foregoing events took place when Malcolm X was still in prison, and he would only be released on August 7, 1952. Yet, his wide reading in prison had made him aware of the events, which obviously had profound effects on the future, ardent Muslim when he became a NOI member, and he subsequently started in the late 1950s to interact with African diplomats at the United Nations, from whom he learned much more. This gave him the ardent desire to visit the Middle East for religious purposes and find the time to travel to Africa for cultural awareness and purposes of nationalist fervor. It was also not surprising that the Honorable Elijah Muhammad's teachings within the NOI about black people, their heritage, and circumstances of enslavement and oppression as well as the fight for civil and human rights caught on very well with Malcolm X, who seemed to be ready to absorb these lessons after his first visit to Chicago in August 1952 in the company of his brothers, who were already ardent NOI members. In fact, Malcolm's visit out of town required permission as he was still on parole from prison. He was not bothered by the inconvenience because following his Islamic conversion he would change his name for the first time from Malcolm Little to Malcolm X, a meaningful event for him since he always thought that his old surname was a slave name.

REVISITING AFRICA AND THE 1964 OAU MEETING

By 1964, Malcolm was still operating from the facts that he had accumulated from the 1950s about African nationalist movements resulting in the desire for frequent visits to Africa, which represented a form of pilgrimage to the motherland. His second 1964 visit to Africa was planned to coincide with the July 1964 annual meeting of heads of state of the Organization of African Unity (OAU). Scheduled for Cairo, Egypt, Malcolm X was admitted as an official observer representing his own Organization of Afro-American Unity (OAAU). This, according to several observers, marked Malcolm's growing internationalism, as he was able on July 7, 1964, to distribute a memorandum to African leaders and other observers, in which he pointed out that the struggle of his fellow blacks in America was over both human and civil rights—and not just civil rights, as Dr. Martin Luther King, Jr. and other leaders of the U.S. civil rights movement were advocating through street protests and marches.

Malcolm X had been fascinated by the establishment of the OAU in 1963, coupled with his admiration for its various purposes and principles, as well as the Banjul Charter on Human and People's Rights, prepared in the Gambian city of Banjul, along with the OAU's Charter on the Rights and Welfare of African Children. Upon the formation of his own organization, Malcolm selected a name for it—the Organization of Afro-American Unity (OAAU)—similar to that of the African continental organization. The purposes and principles of his own OAAU were similar to those of the Organization of African Unity because Malcolm X took the time to study the OAU at its headquarters in Addis Ababa, Ethiopia. He was, indeed, very impressed by the objectives of the OAU enshrined in article II of the overall charter of the organization. For him, anything that united its people was to be regarded as a serious entity; hence the great impression on Malcolm X by the OAU charter's five objectives, which are listed below in alphabetical order:

(a) To promote the unity and solidarity of the African States;

(b) To coordinate and intensify their cooperation and efforts to achieve a better life for the peoples of Africa;

(c) To defend their sovereignty, their territorial integrity and independence;

(d) To eradicate all forms of colonialism from Africa; and

(e) To promote international cooperation, having due regard to the Charter of the United Nations and the Universal Declaration of Human Rights. (From the 1963 OAU Charter as noted by Malcolm X).

Malcolm X had so much respect for the OAU and its leadership that he planned his second visit to Egypt in such a way that it would coincide with the July 17–21, 1964, OAU annual conference that was being held in the capital of Cairo. To make sure that he would not miss anything significant during the OAU heads of state meeting, Malcolm X arrived in Cairo on July 12, 1964, and he checked into the local Semiramis Hotel. Fortuitously, attending the conference that year were African politicians that he had either met before, or with whom he had communicated through letters. Among the first persons he met, before other OAU conference delegates arrived, were Mr. Tom Mboya, the Kenyan political leader; Egyptian Bureau of National Affairs director Hassan S. al-Kholy, who was also a special assistant to then Egyptian president Gamal Abdel Nasser; Angolan rebel leader Jonas Savimbi, who was living in Cairo at the time, and Mrs. Shirley Graham DuBois, the widow of the indomitable Dr. W.E.B. DuBois, who immediately invited Malcolm to dine with her before the conference got under way and became hectic. In fact, Malcolm had met Mrs. DuBois in Ghana during his first visit there (Assensoh and Alex-Assensoh, 2014; Marable 2011).

Malcolm X, as expected, came with his own agenda, which included making sure that his message about the plight of his fellow African Americans back home was spread widely. He was one of those black leaders who were of the opinion that blacks in America were faced with racism to the point of jeopardizing their human rights. Therefore, he also made sure that he secured interviews with major newspapers, radio stations, and other news media outlets. For example, while in Cairo, he was interviewed by a correspondent of *The Observer* newspaper of London as well as United Press International (UPI). As soon as the African leaders arrived and the conference began, Malcolm X was recognized as the leader of the Organization of Afro-American Unity (OAAU) and was invited to serve as a formal observer, a status that enabled him to come closer to the various African leaders and other participants playing active roles in the conference (Jenkins and Tryman 2002; Marable 2011).

As a formal observer, Malcolm X got the opportunity to distribute to the African leaders and other delegates attending the OAU conference in Cairo a written memorandum, in which he strenuously urged countries forming the membership of the OAU to give their support to his efforts accusing the U.S. government before the United Nations of violating the human rights of his fellow blacks in America. In fact, at the time, Malcolm X endeavored to elevate the civil-rights struggles of U.S.-based blacks, led by the late Rev. Dr. Martin Luther King, Jr., to a struggle for human rights in order to seek international support as he contended that the issue at stake was a threat to world or international peace, with Malcolm's alternative vision and hope being "a counter-distinction to that of King and other civil rights leaders" (Jenkins and Tryman 2002, 157).

To persuade the African leaders to support his call to condemn America for the racist way his fellow black men and women were treated in America, Malcolm X endeavored to equate American racism with the prevailing apartheid conditions in South Africa at the time. He contended that racism in the United States was the same as the apartheid situation that African heads of state hated with venom. He further called on the African leaders at the OAU conference to realize that supporting the African Americans in their struggle for dignity and true freedom in the United States was an exhibition of Pan-African politics, hoping that after his African brothers and sisters had fought for freedom from colonialism and imperialism, they would not now become victims of American dollar power. Yet, Malcolm X failed at the Cairo meeting of the OAU to get the African leaders to issue a formal condemnation of the United States of America, as doing so during the Cold War era would have been seen as the African leaders siding ideologically with Russia and other communist countries, (Marable 2011).

Malcolm X, who had succeeded in using correspondence to maintain friendships with several persons in Africa, was not perturbed by the unsuccessful outcome of his memorandum, which was widely circulated at the 1964 OAU annual meeting of the African leaders. Instead, he began to contact several of his friends throughout Africa to urge them to arrange another round of visits to several African countries. In West Africa, he used friends in Ghana and Nigeria to make contacts in the sub-region. For example, his old friend and author, professor E.U. Essien-Udom, who arranged his first visit to Nigeria, was on hand to assist Malcolm this time around. In Ghana, Malcolm used such people as Maya Angelo, the prolific African American writer, Julian Mayfield, himself a well-known author, and T. D. Baffoe, the editor of the influential and government-owned newspaper, *The Ghanaian Times*. To help make contacts for Malcolm's visit to French-speaking West Africa was Paris-based *Presence Africaine* publisher-*cum*-editor Alioune Diop. All of these people helped Malcolm travel to various West African nations, where he was treated royally and like kin, but he did not succeed in persuading any leader in the sub-region to support his anti-American stance, (Marable 2011).

MALCOLM X AND JONAS SAVIMBI, THE UNITA LEADER

It is interesting to note that Malcolm X was not the only organizational leader who was at the annual OAU meeting in Cairo with a personal agenda and frustrated at being unable to achieve his aims. Another such leader, who would briefly befriend him, was the late Jonas Savimbi of Angola, who would later form his own organization known as the National Union for the Total Liberation Independence of Angola or UNITA (Minter 1988). The circumstances were similar to how Malcolm X established his own two organizations in 1964. Initially, Savimbi, with Portuguese and Swiss education, joined Holden Roberto's Union of the Peoples of Angola (UPA), which was at its founding in 1957 called Union of the Peoples Northern Angola. Born on August 3, 1934, at Munhango in the eastern Moxico Province of Angola, Savimbi was from the large Ovimbundu ethnic group, causing Roberto to feel that embracing him in UPA would be beneficial. Roberto's Angola government-in-exile named Savimbi as secretary-general and minister of foreign affairs. Jonas Savimbi became disenchanted with the UPA and so attended the 1964 OAU meeting to speak his peace and to disassociate himself from the UPA (Minter 1988).

At the time of the 1964 OAU meeting, Jonas Savimbi, his Southern African girlfriend, Stella Makunga, and their young daughter (Naniki) lived in Egypt as exiles. He used the presence of the OAU meeting in Cairo to hold a press conference to announce his resignation from UPA by claiming that Roberto was practicing tribal favoritism, and that he was being dictated to by America. Indeed, at the time, it was known that Roberto—who operated from the former Zaire (now DRC)—had been placed on the payroll of the Central Intelligence Agency (CIA) like the then leader Mobutu Seseko and Cecil Adoula. Publicly, Savimbi exposed Roberto at his press conference and flew to Switzerland, where he was an occasional graduate student in order to complete his studies and to earn an equivalent of an American master's degree (*license* in Switzerland) in political science. It was from Switzerland that Savimbi formed his National Union for the Total Liberation and Independence of Angola (UNITA) (Minter 1988).

Malcolm X was present in Cairo when Savimbi openly attacked Holden Roberto making it clear that his Angolan compatriot was an American stooge. Malcolm X was happy to hear and read about that relationship in the Egyptian and international press; it had been claimed in several publications that Roberto allegedly joined Congo's Mobutu and Adoula "on the CIA payroll" (Minter 1988, 6). Interestingly, Malcolm X was to eventually meet with Savimbi, a meeting that would take place outside of

Africa. However, it was to happen too late because, at the time, Savimbi had also been placed on the CIA payroll and so whatever Malcolm X told him was passed on to the American intelligence agencies. Several of the African leaders that Malcolm X met at the 1964 OAU annual meeting were known to be very radical. Yet, they had to be pragmatic and diplomatic in doing anything to undermine America, which provided support for some economic projects in their various countries. For example, although Ghanaian president Kwame Nkrumah was about to have Thomas Nelson and Sons Limited publish *Neo-Colonialism: The Last State of Imperialism*, which came out in 1965 and was considered a blistering attack on the U.S. government in particular and capitalism in general, he still felt obligated to America because the Eisenhower government had supported one of his pet projects, the Volta River project, which culminated in the hydroelectric dam that brought about national electrification. It was widely reported that there was an arrangement agreed upon in 1962 among Ghana's president Kwame Nkrumah as well as Mr. Edgar Kaiser, U.S. president John F. Kennedy, the World Bank, U.S. Exim Bank, the British government, and others that would lead to the construction of the Volta dam and Akosombo power station, which is recorded in British-born James Moxon's book, *Volta: Man's Greatest Lake: The Story of Ghana's Akosombo Dam* (1984) as being like all multi-purpose schemes, the project "has a long history, [which is] well described in this book." (Moxon, 1984, 10).

This collaborative effort (known as the Volta River Project of Ghana) was one of the reasons that president Kwame Nkrumah, as head of the Ghana government, would not support Malcolm X against the U.S. government at the 1964 Organization of African Unity annual meeting in Cairo, Egypt, as it would have jeopardized such large-scale and prosperous economic ventures, which were benefitting Ghana under President Nkrumah's leadership. That was in spite of the fact that Nkrumah, in his Pan-Africanist leanings, had met Malcolm X during his 1964 visit to Ghana. In fact, it has been further shown that the U.S. government's involvement in the Ghana project started before Mr. John F. Kennedy came to the White House as president. It was, indeed, when President Eisenhower was in the White House and began at the time that Mr. Gbedemah, Ghana's finance minister (secretary) had suffered racism at an American restaurant, where he was refused service for being black. He was subsequently invited to the White House by the U.S. president. Discussions then centered on queries about the project, which culminated in a U.S. company and the U.S. government reaching an agreement with the Ghana government on the project. Mr. Edgar F. Kaiser, the head of the American company selected for the contract, reportedly did have a common or mutual interest with Nkrumah to make their project a success but, in the words of Mr. Kaiser, "it wasn't so much that the cut of my hair he [Nkrumah] liked. He liked our money." (Moxon 1969, 288).

After Malcolm's November 14, 1964, disastrous trip to Algeria due to his limitations with the French language, he left for Switzerland to meet some United Nations and other officials that he had encountered at the July 1964 Organization of African Unity annual conference in Cairo. Later on, he talked with Jonas Savimbi, who had impressed Malcolm unlimitedly by blasting Angola's Holden Roberto for being too pro-American before announcing his departure from the FNLA. As stated earlier, Jonas Savimbi also accused Roberto of being on the CIA's payroll. Therefore, when Malcolm X met the UNITA leader, they had frank discussions, during which Malcolm was candid about plans of the OAAU and the Muslim Mosque, Inc.

As some of Savimbi's very close political associates have previously underscored, for the Americans to know what he (Savimbi) and Malcolm X discussed over a period of their friendship, they (the Americans) did their best to "befriend" Savimbi, the charismatic Angolan nationalist leader, who was considered, at the time, to be a very likely future leader of Angola. Before Savimbi was ambushed and killed inside the Angolan jungle, he was alleged to be a paid American agent, similar to the way he previously alleged or accused others. It therefore meant that whatever Malcolm X discussed with him in Geneva could have possibly made its way to the American intelligence or authorities. Whether or not Malcolm X was aware of Savimbi's alleged association with the CIA, he did not regret his visit to Geneva because it also gave him an opportunity to meet other acquaintances or friends he had made or met earlier at the Cairo annual conference of the OAU, including Ned Willard, who was interested in talking with him about the fate of African Americans in America. He also met with an individual that he only names as Fifi, a Swiss national, who happened to be a UN official that he met when he (Malcolm) was in Egypt, and both had had long discussions. After Malcolm's unsuccessful visit to Algeria, he reportedly returned to Geneva to visit one of his friends, Ned Willard.

Savimbi's fortunes seemed to have improved or advanced tremendously in subsequent years when, in April 1974, there was a *coup d'etat* in Lisbon, Portugal, which brought about a change in government. Savimbi's relationship with American officials also did see a lot of improvement. Before that, the American government, reportedly, enjoyed "the dubious distinction of having backed Portuguese colonialism and encouraged the South Africans to invade [Angola] in 1975" (Minter 1988, 22). Jonas Savimbi, like Roberto, was supposed to have benefitted tremendously from the U.S., including having been "openly provided an annual subsidy of over $15 million for Savimbi's contra [UNITA] crusade" (Minter 1988, 22). It was also reported that, at the same time, "the CIA stepped up subsidies to Holden Roberto's FNLA, its long-time client in Zaire, which also gained some aid from China" (Minter 1988, 22). Indeed, Malcolm X would have been unhappy to know that the UNITA leader Savimbi, who had exposed Roberto at the 1964 OAU conference, was alleged to be in the subsequent pay of the Americans through the Central Intelligence Agency (CIA).

Invariably, Malcolm X and Savimbi had a lot in common, as both of them broke away from mainstream religious and political organizations that they were initially associated with to form their own organizations. While Malcolm X's defection was from the Nation of Islam in 1964 leading to the formation of the Organization of Afro American Unity (OAAU) as well as the Muslim Mosque, Inc., Savimbi's defection was from Roberto's FNLA culminating in the establishment of UNITA. The end of Malcolm X stemmed from his assassination in 1965 at the Audubon Ballroom in the heart of his beloved Harlem. British Broadcasting Corporation (BBC) and authentic official Angolan sources confirmed that, after surviving more than a dozen assassination attempts, Savimbi was killed on February 22, 2002, at Lucusse in his birthplace of Moxico Province. He died in the battle between his UNITA forces and Angolan government troops along riverbanks. In the firefight, Savimbi reportedly sustained fifteen gunshot wounds to his head, throat, upper body, and legs. While Savimbi returned fire, his wounds proved fatal as he died at the scene of the fighting.

According to BBC and UNITA information sources, Savimbi was succeeded by Antonio Dembo, who assumed UNITA's leadership on an interim basis in February 2002. However, Dembo had sustained wounds in the same attack that killed Savimbi resulting in his death from the wounds ten days later. He was succeeded by Paulo Lukamba. Six weeks after Savimbi's death, a ceasefire between UNITA and the MPLA was signed but, sadly, Angola remains deeply divided politically between MPLA and UNITA supporters. Parliamentary elections in September 2008 resulted in an overwhelming majority for the MPLA, but their legitimacy was still questioned by UNITA and even international observers.

In the years since Savimbi's death, his legacy has been a source of debate. Several observers, including Alex Vines, who heads the Africa program of the London-based Chatham House, argue that the huge mistake that Savimbi made was to reject the election and go back to the Angolan bush to continue the devastating civil war. Furthermore, several scholars and observers of Angolan military science, including University of Oxford's expert Paula Roque, have underscored that Savimbi was, indeed, a very charismatic man, who exuded power and leadership. Therefore, in their estimation, one cannot easily forget that—for a large segment of the Angolan population back in Africa—his UNITA forces did represent something tangible and respectable, especially since Savimbi came from the Ovimbundu, one of the largest Angolan ethnic or tribal groups, which was the reason behind Holden Roberto's decision to invite him to the NFLA and make him one of his top advisors. After all, in African politics, one's ethnicity (or tribe) could help to advance one's political fortunes.

In terms of Savimbi's relationship with Malcolm X, it is felt that if both of them were alive, there was the likelihood that they would still be friends until it became evident that the Angolan warlord was, indeed, in the pay of the American Central Intelligence Agency (CIA), as it has often been alleged. For example, In *Defending the Spirit: A Black Life in America*, TransAfrica founder and president Randall Robinson, has reiterated that after Portugal retreated from Angola, "the United States under the guiding hand of Secretary of State Henry Kissinger threw its military support behind the Angolan guerrilla leader Jonas Savimbi, who with the further support of white minority-led South Africa was intent on overthrowing the new and widely recognized government in Luanda, now assisted in its defense by Cuban forces" (Robinson 1998, 175). While other claims about Savimbi's collision course with American intelligence systems, spearheaded by the CIA, were deemed speculative and inclusive, Robinson—a lawyer who influenced American public opinion against apartheid-South Africa and also helped to influence U.S. policies toward Africa and the Caribbean—knew what he was writing about. However, it would have been questionable as to whether Malcolm X would have closed his eyes to such pieces of credible information and continue to interact with Jonas Savimbi, more so as he was always very sensitive to and suspicious of American officialdom.

What would have irked Malcolm more was the fact that Savimbi was an ally of apartheid South Africa, which had suppressed, maimed, and murdered several of the country's nationalist leaders, including Steve Biko, and during Malcom X' life had incarcerated the lawyer Nelson Mandela, who later became the first black president of South Africa.

TransAfrica President Randall Robinson went on to substantiate some of these facts. For example, he lamented the fact that the Angolan government of President Jose Eduardo dos Santos had been recognized by African countries as well as even the conservative government of then prime minister Margaret Thatcher. Yet, as he bluntly puts it, Savimbi was eventually supported by the Americans (Robinson 2011).

CHAPTER 3

MALCOLM X'S FORAY
IN EAST AFRICA

Malcolm X's trip to East Africa in the fall of 1964 held a special significance for him. As planned, he was initially to arrive in Nairobi, the Kenyan capital. From there, he would visit other East African geographic areas. Although East Africa was not new to Malcolm at this time, it was a fact that he was not aware of certain dynamics. According to the available records, Malcolm arrived in Nairobi in the first week of October 1964 from the Middle East. As Marika Sherwood has confirmed in her very useful book, *Malcolm X: Visits Abroad, April 1964–February 1965*, at the time of his arrival in Kenya, it was a nation with a total population that was very close to nine million people.

In varied ways, Malcolm X held in high esteem Kenya's Kikuyu ethnic group, from among whom then president Jomo Kenyatta emerged as one of the foremost Kenyan nationalist leaders to lead the anti-colonial struggle. He also had high regard for Tom Mboya's Luo ethnic group, which had produced the vice-president of the country, Oginga Odinga. It must be noted that Malcolm X regarded the Kenyan tumultuous anti-colonial struggle known as *Mau Mau* as a true revolution (in contrast to his assessment of the civil rights movement of the USA, with its pro-Gandhian non-violent philosophy). As Sherwood disclosed, in the case of Tom Mboya, Malcolm was impressed that he had risen through the cabinet ranks of Kenya; for example, at independence, Tom Mboya was initially made minister for labor; then, in 1963, he was moved to the Justice and Constitutional Affairs Ministry and, in1964, when president Jomo Kenyatta declared Kenya as a republic, Mboya was again moved to a new ministry, this time to serve as the minister of economic planning and development, as reported in Sherwood's book (Sherwood 2011, 82).

From all accounts, Malcolm's second visit to Kenya was much different from his first visit to the East African nation, with the first visit being more of a tourist attraction. However, his second visit had a pilgrimage factor, as he wanted to meet as many political leaders as possible. Therefore, with the help of Mboya, appointments were made for him to meet Kenyan President Kenyatta, vice-president Oginga Odinga, and other top leaders, several of whom were happy that they were playing hosts to a brother from the black diaspora in America.

Upon Malcolm's arrival on October 5, 1964, it was arranged for him to visit some tourist attractions, during which time he was informed that Vice-President Odinga was ready to meet with him. He was very impressed with the second most important Kenyan leader, Mr. Oginga, as he underscored in his diary that, although advanced in age, Mr. Oginga Odinga paid rapt attention to details of their discussions, which centered on African-Afro-American relations. It was decided at the meeting with the Kenyan vice-president that Malcolm X would address the Kenyan National Parliament on October 15, 1964. Since Malcolm X had to wait for about a week before addressing the Kenyan legislative assembly, he decided to travel to Tanzania, where he planned to visit the island of Zanzibar, which teamed up with Tanganyika to form the combined name of the new nation. Having also met Tanzanian leaders at the annual meeting of the defunct OAU, Malcolm was anxious to renew ties with them at home. In fact, the main person Malcolm was anxious to meet was his fellow Muslim, Abdulrrahman Muhammad Babu.

Indeed, many facts about Babu did impress as well as intrigue Malcolm X. Like Malcolm, Babu was a founder of a viable 1963 political organization in his country, the Umma Party of Zanzibar. Before that, between 1957 and 1963, he had served as the secretary-general of what was then known as the Zanzibar Nationalist Party. Apart from earlier serving as minister of planning, Babu served his country as foreign minister, in fact before Malcolm X was to visit Tanzania, from January 1964 to April 1964. Malcolm X learned that Babu was one of the leading Zanzibari intellectuals, who were jostling for both power and prominence in the early 1960s, an unfortunate situation that led to the fall out between the intellectuals and Sheik Abeid Amani Karume, who was leading the Zanzibar Revolutionary Council. The tussle turned bloody in Zanzibari politics, as Karume was assassinated in 1972 while serving as the president of the tiny Zanzibari island. For the death of the charismatic Karume, Babu and over thirty other local intellectuals were arrested, tried, and sentenced to death while about two dozen other alleged conspirators were found not guilty and released.

To many observers, the death of Karume did pave the way for the unification of Tanganyika and Zanzibar. So, in the observance of the fourteenth anniversary of the unification of Tanganyika and Zanzibar in April 1978, president Julius K. Nyerere released Babu and several of the convicted prisoners, who had been found guilty of the assassination of Karume. After his release, Babu decided to stay outside Tanzania settling in the United Kingdom, where he was elected by the Board of the Africa Center of London to serve as its chairman from 1985 to 1989.

During Malcolm X's October 1964 visit to Tanzania, Babu played a major role in hosting his fellow Muslim, when Babu was in center stage. For example, Malcolm has noted in his travelogue inscriptions that Babu arranged for him to see other like-minded brothers, including those that Babu brought to visit with him on October 12 in his hotel.

Among scheduled events was an interview that Malcom X agreed to give exclusively to the *Nationalist* publication. The interview prompted the American Embassy, in its reports about Malcolm's Tanzanian visit, to inform the United States Department of State that the black Muslim from the USA was rapping on the doors of Africa. When Babu took him to visit his home region and island of Zanzibar, the embassy showed keen interest and wondered how long Malcom would stay in Tanzania. It was on October 13, 1964, that Malcolm visited Babu's home to have dinner with him and his family.

It was during Malcolm X's visit to Babu's home that he was told that he would have the opportunity of meeting president Julius K. Nyerere at 6:00 p.m. on October 15. While with Babu, they discussed matters of mutual interest in the Islamic world as well as current affairs. The day arrived, and Babu kept his promise to take Malcolm to see President Nyerere. It was on that day that communist China became the fifth nation to explode a nuclear bomb. It was no longer a secret because U.S. President Johnson confirmed that the Chinese had detonated what was described as a low-yield atomic bomb. However, Chairman Mao's country did caution the world not to underestimate the military significance of the bomb's test.

In spite of the warning, experts estimated at the time that it would take between four and ten years for the Chinese to have the capability to develop an operational nuclear delivery system. It was at that same time that the Soviet Premier Nikita Khrushchev was removed from office. The nuclear test event boosted Chinese standing in the communist world, something that Malcom X watched with a keen interest. In discussions, Malcolm learned that Chairman Mao's China apparently did not, at the time, have the ability to produce large amounts of plutonium, which was supposed to be the bomb's fissionable material. As Malcolm learned in some detail, several experts did hold the speculation that the testing of the bombing device was an expensive but a prestigious project for communist China. The prediction was that between three and four years, the Chinese scientists would be able to develop bombs with such compactness that they could be moved around much more easily. Malcolm, Babu, and some Tanzanian political leaders enjoyed discussing several nuances about the Chinese atomic bombing process.

However, it was obvious that the explosion of the nuclear device, while Malcolm was in Tanzania, did catch several experts off guard, although it was on record that, about a month earlier in September of 1964, the U.S. secretary of state Dean Rusk had announced that the United States was aware of China's nuclear capabilities, and that it was expected that the Chinese could test their first atomic bomb in the near future. History professor Richard E. Pipes, and other experts on China, including professor William Blackwell of New York University (NYU) had speculated, on their own, that the Chinese event and the Soviet removal of Kruschev from office would lead to closer ties among leaders of the communist world. Above all, Professor Pipes underscored the fact that the Chinese nuclear test would add to the prestige of the Chinese communist leadership and strengthen Chinese bargaining position in the world.

Meanwhile Babu noted that when Malcolm X met President Nyerere, Dr. Nyerere saw the nuclear bomb test by China in ideological terms. Dr. Marika Sherwood quoted the Tanzanian leader as saying to Malcolm X: "Malcolm, for the first time today in recorded history, a former colonial country has been able to develop weapons at par with any colonial power. This is the end of colonialism through and through" (Sherwood 2011, 78).

In his own response, Malcolm X reportedly told President Nyerere that, on his way to see him, he was in fact thinking about the Chinese testing of the nuclear bomb. However, Dr. Sherwood did disclose through her own research that Malcolm X, at that point, had the avowed interest to promote internationalism among Third World nations and leaders, including how one could mobilize and organize Third World populations in America, thoughts which separated Malcolm X from other black leaders, who were singularly interested in civil rights issues rather than a focus on international ones. Interestingly, Babu did his best to make Malcolm feel at home in Tanzania, but it was also a fact that he was not the only person interested in welcoming the African American into their community. They included several African Americans and other Africans. One of them was Ed Anderson, who later wrote Malcolm X: "We greatly appreciated your recent visit to Dar-es-Salaam. Your influence on the minds and hearts of the people that heard your message cannot be measured. You left a host of followers and well-wishers behind..." (Sherwood 2011; 78–79).

Between October 14 and 15, 1964, Malcolm X was scheduled to meet with Tanzanian foreign minister Oscar Kambona and later leave for Nairobi, Kenya. When he learned from Kambona that a four-leader conference was to take place in Tanzania among Jomo Kenya (Kenya), Kenneth Kaunda (Zambia), Milton Obote (Uganda), and Nyerere (Tanzania), he decided to postpone his departure. Over dinner with Kambona, Malcolm learned that the four heads of state were to discuss the Congo crisis and efforts to ensure that Mozambique and Southern Rhodesia (now Zimbabwe) would gain their own independence. There was also to be the meeting of the African Liberation Committee in Dar-es-Salaam when Malcolm was still there. However, Malcolm was not invited to these meetings. While the meetings were going on among the four Eastern African leaders as well as among members of the African Liberation Committee, Malcolm X arranged a visit to the Cuban Embassy in Dar-es-Salaam to speak with Ambassador Rodriguez, an Afro-Cuban career diplomat. It was obvious that Malcolm made such contacts to infuriate the American political leaders because U.S.-Cuban relations were at their lowest ebb. For example, his visit to the Cuban Embassy was a mere courtesy call, but he made it seem as if it was for some strategic reasons. An interesting scenario was that, as Malcolm X was leaving Tanzania for Kenya, he fortuitously found himself in the midst of two of the very leaders whose meetings he was not invited to attend.

On the plane from Tanzania to Kenya were Kenyan President Kenyatta and President Obote of Uganda. Since Malcolm knew several Kenyan officials from his attendance of the OAU annual meeting in Egypt, one of such officials spotted him and immediately introduced him to Kenyatta and Obote. Without hesitation, the two African leaders invited Malcolm to sit near them to have a chat with him. President Kenyatta, who knew that Malcolm was going to stay in Kenya for some days, promised to see him again. Soon after that brief encounter, the plane arrived in Mombasa, where Kenyatta alighted and spend the night, while Malcolm and Obote continued their discussions up to Nairobi international airport, which was later renamed in honor of President Kenyatta. Throughout the trip, Obote and Malcolm engaged in some important discussions about blacks in America until they arrived at the Jomo Kenyatta International Airport (which was formerly called Embakasi Airport).

Although it was in 1964 that the Ugandan president Milton Obote and Malcolm X met on the flight from Tanzania, interestingly, it was common knowledge that a year earlier, in 1963, Dr. Obote had communicated with the Kennedy administration about what he, as an African leader, saw as an appalling treatment of African Americans in the United States. As expected, Malcolm was impressed with the airport, which happens to be Kenya's largest aviation facility, and the busiest airport in East Africa. Its importance as an aviation center makes it a major player when it comes to airports in the region, especially as the Jomo Kenyatta International Airport daily serves an average of nineteen thousand passengers from Africa, Europe, and Asia. Malcolm X did observe that Kenya deserved commendation for such a nice airport. Arriving there, he was picked up that day by Tom Mboya, a senior member of President Kenyatta's government, for the close to 14–17 kilometer journey to downtown Nairobi, indeed into the business district.

Apart from holding discussions with Mboya, who was once the head of the Federation of Labor, Malcolm visited the Equator Club in Nairobi. There, Malcolm met several elite Kenyan leaders, including other cabinet members. Dr. Njoroge Mungai, the then health minister, was there to speak with Malcolm. He also had the opportunity to meet top Kenyan leaders such as then vice-president Oginga Odinga and, eventually, president Jomo Kenyatta, both of whom received him with open arms as the leader of the Organization of Afro-American Unity (OAAU), with its headquarters in the USA (Sherwood 2011).

Malcolm had the opportunity to address the Kenyan Parliament on October 15, 1964, an event that he considered very important, as he used that opportunity to reiterate his call for continental Africans to join him and other diaspora-based blacks to condemn America for its racism against the black population in America. However, the greatest day for Malcolm in Kenya was on October 20, 1964, the day that he was picked up from his Nairobi hotel (Equator Inn) by Mr. and Mrs. Pamela Mboya for the sole purpose of meeting President Kenyatta. He was treated as a visitor with VIP status; the Mboyas took Malcolm to a parade at which President Kenyatta was scheduled to speak, and he was seated not far from the Kenyan leader with only his daughter, Jane Kenyatta, sitting between the two. Malcolm wrote in his travelogue, which is available for research purposes, that President Kenyatta's address that evening included references to the *Mau Mau* movement, which was used as a nationalist organization to spearhead the struggle for Kenyan independence by the black nationalist leaders when Kenyatta was, in fact, in jail. That evening, Malcolm joined the Kenyattas, the Mboyas, and other dignitaries for dinner, during which time he claimed that wine was served, and he did drink some despite being a Muslim (Marable 2011).

American diplomats in East Africa keenly watched and listened to Malcolm X during his visits to Tanzania and Kenya. They were shocked that at interviews—including one that he gave to Kenya television journalists on October 21, 1964—he used the opportunity to blast the American government and, characteristically, called on his hosts to hold America accountable for racism against his fellow blacks. What surprised many observers, at the time, was that Malcolm had quickly forgotten that he failed, at the 1964 OAU annual meeting of African leaders, to get the African leaders to condemn the United States publicly. Malcolm was intrigued by the fact that fellow black employees of the United States Information Service (USIS, now called United States Information

Agency, USIA) were used to counteract his own anti-USA propaganda by spreading like a wild bush fire the news of the passing of the 1964 Civil Rights Act by the president Lyndon B. Johnson administration. By dwelling on the passage of the Civil Rights Act, the East Africa-based American officials showed that the American government was doing its best for blacks in America, including Malcolm X, who was giving the impression that he and his fellow blacks of the United States were still being subjected to Jim Crow and other discriminatory laws. It was explained explicitly overseas that the new act was enacted to take effect on July 2, 1964, to enforce the constitutional right to vote, to confer jurisdiction upon the district courts of the United States of America to provide injunctive relief against discrimination in public accommodations as well as to authorize the American attorney-general to institute suits to protect the constitutional rights in public facilities and public education, to extend the existing Commission on Civil Rights, to prevent discrimination in federally-assisted programs, and to establish an Equal Employment Opportunity Commission (EEOC).

Malcolm still wished that he could persuade African political leaders with whom he spoke in East Africa to join his anti-American crusade because, at the time, he did not see anything good in American laws geared toward the civil rights of blacks. This time around, he began speaking about the lack of human rights, wishing that the United Nations could, as well, be persuaded to join his campaign against the United States by allowing a discussion of the plight of African Americans, many of whom had opted, since the mid-1830s, to leave American shores for the Republic of Liberia in West Africa.

In fact, at the time Malcolm X was fuming in East Africa about USIA propaganda aimed at countering his own anti-USA sentiments, Liberia was under the tight grip of the leadership of president William V.S. Tubman, whose ancestry originated among the so-called Americo-Liberian ethnic group of American blacks, who migrated to the West African nation. As professor Claude Andrew Clegg, III of Indiana University has attested to in his book, *Price of Liberty*, the freed slaves from America went to Liberia and lorded over this country and the indigenous Kru, Vai, Grebo, Bassa, and other ethnic populations. They in fact had a motto, "Love of Liberty Brought Us Here," which the native Liberians considered offensive. That was why the native Liberians, in converse, had their own motto: "Love of Liberty met us here" (Clegg 1997, x).

Malcolm X was, indeed, aware of the autocratic leadership of the Liberia-based Americo-Liberians because he had previously visited Liberia and, in November 1964, was scheduled to return to the country. He would eventually visit Liberia from November 6–9, 1964, but would not be able to have an audience with President Tubman, not even when he visited his Executive Mansion (an equivalent of the American President's White House) to meet the country's cabinet (Marable 2011, 384).

Although Malcolm X was in East Africa, he still remembered that he was scheduled to travel back to Liberia in November before leaving finally to return to the United States. Malcolm looked forward to this Liberian trip because he knew the historic facts about how freed slaves of America returned to the West African nation as Americo-Liberians to help build the country, whose capital of Monrovia was named in 1823 in honor of President James Monroe, the fifth U.S. president from March 4, 1817, to March 4, 1825. Malcolm was excited by the information that President Monroe was, in fact, honored in Liberia because President Monroe supported the rebuilding and subsequent establishment of Liberia by the Americo-Liberians as we know it today.

Although most world leaders in the 1800s were considered in colonialist and imperialist terms, Malcolm X was also aware of the fact that at the time that Monrovia was being named in Monroe's honor, the American leader in the same year (1823) was opposing any European power that tried to intervene imperialistically in the newly established independent nations in the Third World through his Monroe Doctrine, a major American governmental policy. Interestingly, as an individual who read widely, Malcolm X had read from history books that Monroe's presidency did bring about the conclusion of the first period of American presidential history, which was certainly before the beginning of what is widely known as Jacksonian democracy and the ushering in of the two-party system of American political governance. Monroe retired from politics in 1825, and he died on July 4, 1831, in New York City.

While Malcolm X was engrossed with his pending November 1964 trip to Liberia, he flew from Kenya, toward the end of October 1964, to Addis Ababa, the capital of Ethiopia, which a year earlier in March 1963 had welcomed the establishment of the headquarters of the Organization for African Unity (OAU), from whose name he appeared to have adapted his own Organization for Afro-American Unity (OAAU). Having also read much about emperor Haile Selassie and his war with the Italians, Malcolm was interested in a visit to his country to see if he would be able to meet some important local politicians as well as OAU officials there, especially some of the leaders whose acquaintance he had made at the OAU annual meeting in Cairo in the summer of 1964. From the available records, Malcolm had the opportunity to meet only a few Ethiopian leaders and some administrative staff employees of the OAU.

Malcolm was also interested in visiting Addis Ababa at this time because he wanted to meet the former United Nations representative of Guinea, Diallo Telli, who was friends with him when Telli represented Guinea from September 1958 to June 1964, before formally resigning to be secretary-general of the OAU in Ethiopia, serving in that capacity from July 1964 to the early 1970s. Malcolm was fascinated by the fact that when he talked with Telli at the United Nations, a few years earlier, he had learned that he and Telli were born in the same year (1925). Now that Telli was heading the most important African organization, he thought that he might be able to talk directly with him about the racism that confronted him and other African Americans in the United States.

Unfortunately, Ambassador Telli was tied up with crucial OAU business, so Malcolm X had to settle for some of his deputies, with whom he discussed African and African American issues. He was also happy when one of the deputies said that Ambassador Telli had arranged for Malcolm to meet Ghana-born economist, Dr. Robert Atta Gardiner, who was from 1961 to 1975 the executive secretary of the United Nation's Addis Ababa-based Economic Commission for Africa (ECA). He had assumed the UN-affiliate position with a lot of experience, including that of having worked previously as the head of Ghana's civil service as well as serving as a deputy executive secretary for ECA, with secondment as officer-in-charge for the UN operation in the Congo. The author of *Development of Social Administration*, Dr. Gardiner, succeeded the Sudanese-born Mr. Mekki Abbas as ECA boss. Mekki Abbas was himself the first ECA executive secretary from 1959 to 1961, the year that Gardiner succeeded him.

Malcolm X and Dr. Gardiner got on very well, as they had ample time to discuss the plight of African Americans in America. Having served the United Nations in New York before, Dr. Gardiner was aware of the racism accusation that Malcolm X leveled against the current and previous American administrations. Gardiner did express surprise that America, in spite of the civil rights movement that Rev. Dr. Martin Luther King, Jr. had strongly and successfully led, there was still lingering racism facing Malcolm X and his kith and kin, as Dr. Gardiner saw all blacks in America as being kinsfolk. Malcolm X was impressed that Dr. Gardiner had the time to listen to him, and he left the ECA head office in Addis Ababa deeply satisfied.

It is interesting that Dr. Gardiner took the discussions about racism very seriously. This is borne out by the fact that his first talk in the six Reith Lecture Series, which had an overall theme of "World of People" and started on Sunday, November 7, 1965, had as the topic, "Racism." In that lecture, Dr. Gardiner analyzed what he saw as the attitudes that contributed to racism and explored the reasons for racial discrimination. He posed the question: "If repulsion is not instinctive and strangeness is not the cause of antagonism, then why and how does racial resentment arise?" To answer the question he reviewed the characteristics of racism, ending with an abhorrence of racism in general. This did not surprise anyone who knew that Dr. Gardiner and Malcolm X did meet to discuss the subject of racism the previous year, except that listeners to the British Broadcasting Corporation (BBC) could not believe that Dr. Gardiner would utilize such an important occasion to discuss the topic of racism, since he knew that the annual BBC lectures dwelt on significant contemporary issues by those eminently qualified in their relevant fields.

It is unfortunate that Malcolm X could not meet Diallo Telli as he could not have known that his friend and OAU's first secretary-general (whom Malcolm knew very well at the UN headquarters when Telli represented Guinea, headed by president Sekou Toure) was destined to die gruesomely in 1977 at a prison known as Camp Boiro in Guinea. As stated in a previous chapter, Telli, who held very important positions in Guineau after his six-year ambassadorship at the United Nations and as OAU secretary-general for over a decade, was reportedly arrested on July 18, 1976, at his home and imprisoned at Camp Boiro. Unfortunately for Telli, it was Mamadi Keita, the brother-in-law of President Toure, that was selected to head the commission of inquiry that condemned him to death for, allegedly, leading a plot by Fulanis against the Toure government in Guinea.

Although Ambassador Telli's French education included law, he was reportedly subjected to intense interrogations, torture, and an inadequate diet. Allegedly, after the second round of his torture session, Telli was so shattered that he agreed to sign a "confession" that claimed that he had committed treason. Journalists, who saw the written confession, described its incoherence, even after it had been edited by the tribunal. It is reported that, in February 1977, Telli was one of five prominent Guinean prisoners killed through torture at the camp, where they suffered what was alleged to be the "black diet," which meant no food or water. They included ex-Guinean cabinet members B. Alpha Oumar, Drame Alioune, and army officers Diallo Alhassana and Kouvate Lamine. Many observers wondered what Malcolm would have done had he been alive and learned that Ambassador Telli, his very great acquaintance, faced such a fate at the hands of the very regime that he had served very faithfully in the past. It was also surprising that the OAU did not react to the brutal murder of its first secretary general. However, the sudden disappearance from Guinean politics of such a well-respected, international diplomat, who was known for his dignity and good nature, did obviously show clearly that President Toure's government was not as progressive as socialist supporters made it seem to be.

In fact, when Malcolm X visited Ghana on more than one occasion, including a final visit in 1965 on his way back to the United States from East Africa, he was highly impressed with the leadership of then president Kwame Nkrumah, who spent six years as a political exile (from 1966 to 1972) in Guinea after his elected government was overthrown in the February 24, 1966, *coup d'etat* led by military and police officers of his own armed forces. Observers have wondered what Nkrumah would have done if he was still in Guinea when Telli was arrested and detained. With great respect for Ambassador Telli and his family, Nkrumah could have intervened on his behalf. He could at least have insisted on a truly independent commission of inquiry to try to establish his true guilt. However, Diallo Telli's cruel end happened after Nkrumah's death in 1972 and, indeed, a dozen years after Malcolm's own assassination. Since Malcolm visited Liberia and Guinea together in early November 1964 and had cordial discussions with President Toure, many observers felt that Malcolm—in 1977 at the age of fifty-two—would have been able to fly to Guinea to plead with Toure to spare the life of Telli, whom he considered to be a personal friend from their long United Nations association and interactions and several meetings through New York-based social circles. Malcolm X, in November 1965, decided to return to America, as professor Manning Marable has reported, "By the beginning of November 1965, Malcolm had been away from the United States for four months" (Marable 2011, 392).

CHAPTER 4

MALCOLM X AS ALHAJI (EL-HAJ) MALIK EL-SHABAZZ

During Malcolm X's visits to Africa, among his trump cards was the fact that he had embraced the Islamic religion of which many Africans were a part. For example, he hit it well in Tanzania because the main politician, who was playing host and calling shots for him—including facilitating his meeting with president Julius K. Nyerere—was Mohamed Abdulrahman Babu, a fellow Muslim from the island of Zanzibar, another place Malcolm X visited. Interestingly, Babu, who was a cabinet minister in the Nyerere regime in Tanzania, was only a year older than Malcolm X, as Babu was born in 1924 in Zanzibar, one of the British protectorates in East Africa, which later became part of Tanzania when it gained its independence. Malcolm saw a copy of Babu's autobiographical sketch that was to constitute the memoirs a publisher had accepted for publication. The sketch was to help Malcolm produce his autobiography, a book which was to debate the notion of African socialism.

Being a Muslim like Malcolm X, Babu was deeply steeped in Zanzibari politics, which was at the time being led by Islamic leaders on the island. Again, as stated in an earlier chapter, Malcolm had read that Babu was among the leading intellectual members of the Afro-Shirazzi Party, which opposed island leader Sheik Abeid Karume's Zanzibar Revolutionary Council.

Upon the historic merger between Tanganyika and Zanzibar in 1964, Malcolm's friend Babu was serving as secretary of the Zanzibar Nationalist Party (and was among the progressive, leftist members of the Zanzibari government) and was in the running for a top cabinet position. During this time, Babu was known to have maintained a very close relationship with the Chinese leadership in Beijing, a close association that made him one of the leading East African politicians to pay an official visit in 1959 to Chairman Mao's communist China. As a writer, he did some work for the New China News Agency, a professional association that grew into ideological facets. In fact, Malcolm X was known to have a lot of interest in China, as he was known to quote Chinese leaders in some of his public utterances back in Harlem in the 1960s.

It was not surprising that his Islamic friend, Babu, had strong Chinese ties, which would benefit Tanzania as a whole. For example, Babu played a major role in the establishment of a local railway project that was known as the Tarzarfa Railways, constructed with Chinese assistance. Since president Julius Nyerere wanted to utilize the existing Zanzibar ties with China, through Babu, he selected him to head a delegation, with trade interests, to visit China, before Nyerere's own presidential delegation went to China in 1964. Malcolm X was very happy to know about the very beneficial and tangible relationship that Babu had created between China and his home country of Tanzania. The speculation was that if Malcolm X had not died prematurely in 1965, he would have used Babu to cultivate a Chinese relationship that could have benefitted his organizations: Organization of Afro-American Unity and Muslim Mosque, Inc.

It was, therefore, coincidental that the Federal Bureau of Investigation (FBI) director J. Edgar Hoover was ahead of his game by suspecting Malcolm X, Martin Luther King, Jr., and several other black leaders of the civil rights movement as having communist connections, even before they materialized. For Malcolm, his meeting with Babu and other socialist leaders on the African continent did spur a fascination for socialism, but there was nothing to confirm that he already had *bona fide* socialist connections at the time of his assassination in 1965. Malcolm X confirmed this in his posthumously published memoir, *Autobiography of Malcolm X* (written with Alex Haley), where he likened his trips to Africa to a pilgrimage, whereby he felt special in the midst of his fellow blacks, but this time in a different setting: in the motherland (Africa)! Although Malcolm's visits in East Africa were well received by both Muslim and Christian brothers and sisters, it was obviously clear that he was much more at home with individuals who would invite him to mosques to pray to his favorite Allah. That was where the Tanzanian political genius, Babu, was supremely helpful.

The enigmatic aspect of Malcolm's life, however, underscored that he was also at home with non-Muslim brothers in some African venues. For example, in contrast to what happened in Tanzania, where Babu played a central role in Malcolm X's successful visit to that nation, it was a different picture in some of the West African countries that he visited. In Nigeria, Malcolm's successful visits there—on two separate occasions— were spearheaded by a non-Muslim, professor E. Essien-Udom. The interesting scenario is that Dr. Essien-Udom, on whom Malcolm heavily relied for his knowledge of West African affairs, had deep-rooted U.S. connections that Malcolm appreciated. In other words, whether he was a Muslim or not, Malcolm trusted the judgment of anyone who would expand his horizon on Africa.

Professor Essien-Udom was three years younger than Malcolm X, as he was born in October 1928. As discussed in an earlier chapter, he had benefitted from a Fulbright-Hays award to study and earn his political science degree in 1955 at Oberlin College in Ohio, USA, then went on to pursue graduate studies at University of Chicago (1955–1961) with the usual graduate fellowships and teaching assistantships. Upon the completion of his doctoral (PhD) degree in political science (with a specialization in international relations) from University of Chicago, he served on various American campuses, including Harvard and Brown universities. As a patriot (he returned home to Nigeria to lecture at the University of Ibadan between 1965 and 1988), Essien-Udom rose to the rank of full professor, serving as the dean of the social sciences faculty, before he left the University of Ibadan campus to serve as the founding vice-chancellor of University of Maiduguri in Nigeria. It was, in fact, while researching for materials to complete a book in the early 1960s that he came in contact with Malcolm X in New York, and they became fast friends. His manuscript was published as *Black Nationalism: a Search for Identity in America*, a copy of which he autographed for Malcolm, and of which he was very proud.

Professor Essien-Udom, some of his faculty colleagues, and his wife (Mrs. Ruby Essien-Udom) planned and executed the successful visit of Malcolm X to Nigeria. His students and colleagues at University of Ibadan reportedly gave him the nickname of "Black Power Professor," an accolade that he treasured. With strong diasporic-black ties to Malcom X and some of Marcus Garvey's kinfolk, Professor Essien-Udom co-edited, with Mrs. Amy Jacques Garvey, *More Philosophy and Opinions of Marcus Garvey*. Apart from his strong ties to Malcolm X, he was also influenced by the tenets of Pan-Africanism and Garveyism. It was not surprising that the military government of his native South Eastern State of Nigeria, between 1973 and 1975, tapped him to serve as its secretary. Upon his death, Essien-Udoh was survived by Mrs. Ruby Essien-Udom as well as his children, other relatives, and friends. Although Dr. Essien-Udom was not a Muslim *per se*, one can see how his illustrious U.S. academic background made his relationship with Malcom X both *bona fide* and mutually beneficial. He gained Malcolm's assistance for contacts and other information needs each time the Nigerian scholar visited the United States to complete research for his important book. Of course, Malcolm X did not take his Islamic obligations lightly; hence, while in Egypt and on his way to perform his initial pilgrimage to Mecca, he accepted religious instruction from Islamic clerics of what professor Manning Marable described as the Cairo-based Supreme Council for Islamic Affairs (SCIA) (Marable 2011).

With his enigmatic personality, Malcom X surprised observers with his actions in a variety of ways, including those who served as his friends. For example, during his first visit to Ghana and upon his return to the West African nation, he was welcomed enthusiastically by African American residents of Accra, including Maya Angelou and Dr. Shirley Graham DuBois, who entertained him. During the 1964 OAU annual meeting in Cairo, Egypt, he was also well received by Julian Mayfield, St. Clair Drake, and professor Leslie Alexander Lacy. Lacey's twenty-two-page 1971 book about the 1966 Ghana coup ousting President Nkrumah and his CPP regime was considered curious by Dr. Drake and others. The book, *The Rise and Fall of a Proper Negro*, had been published by Pocket Books. The friends in Ghana were not Muslims, but Malcolm X felt very much at home as well. Indeed, he had no suspicions of his hosts but, as professor Kevin K. Gaines of University of Michigan has underscored, "When in Accra, Malcolm's conversations with black Americans [African Americans] contained indications of the danger that awaited him back at home" (Gaines 2006, 196).

Above all, it is very significant to note that Malcolm X knew the importance of the Muslim titles he had earned by dint of hard work, including performing the required *Hajj* in the Holy Land. Therefore, there was ample justification when his name, from its original Malcolm Little, saw a reincarnation and, by the time he was cut down suddenly by an assassin's bullet in February 1965, Malcolm X had also inherited his Muslim name of El-Hajj Malik el-Shabazz. His wife—who also followed her husband's hard work ethic—returned to college to earn degrees from the University of Massachusetts and became Dr. Betty Shabazz.

CHAPTER 5

MALCOLM X: A
GROWING FASCINATION
AND AN ASSESSMENT

Although Malcolm X has been dead since 1965 and, in fact in 2015, his admirers in and outside the United Sates picked the chance to celebrate half of a century of his death with pomp, gaiety, and circumstance, there is still a growing fascination about his life and all that he represented as a black man in the context of African history as well as being an African American and a black Muslim preacher and leader. Most certainly, there is a reason for the seeming resurgence, which has included American officialdom finding it necessary to put the effigy and name of Malcolm X on a stamp of the U.S. Postal Service. The launching was praised by his oldest daughter, Attallah Shabazz.

From historical-*cum*-political perspectives, one can conclude that Malcolm's image is not being refurbished now at random. Instead, it started several years ago, especially as Americans from all walks of life started to assess the man and what he represented in general. Malcolm X's Pan-Africanist move has not been heralded very much, considering that he deemed it necessary toward the end of his life to spend several months in Africa to break bread with various political and community leaders on the continent. It is confirmed from Malcolm's carefully noted travelogue/diary—available at the Schomburg and also noted in professor Manning Marable's *Malcolm X: A Life of Reinvention* (2011)—that from April of 1964 to November of that year, Malcolm X was out of America, mostly visiting Africa (Marable 2011, 374). This is why, in the months leading to his death by an assassin's bullet, many black men and women, as part of the grassroots, have shown what they considered to be an awareness of the various transformations that Malcolm X went through in the 1960s. At the time, many black men and women were fascinated by the new Malcolm, so they followed the changes in him with much interest and fascination. There was also ample time for Americans to start to debate several issues about the man, including his Nation of Islam (NOI) problems, which had been heightened by a rift with the Honorable Elijah Muhammad, a leader whom he had previously worshipped but whom he held in contempt due to moral lapses identified by Malcolm.

Internationally, Malcolm X was in tune with several Pan-Africanist leaders as well as diaspora-based blacks. Indeed, at the time, an event in which both USA- and Africa-based blacks showed great convergence was certainly in the way Malcom X, the Rev. Dr. Martin Luther King, Jr., Dr. W.E.B. DuBois, and others saw things with respect to the Vietnam War. Writing as editors in the 287-page book, *W.E.B. DuBois on Africa* (2012), University of Miami professors Eugene F. Provenzo, Jr. and Edmund Abaka praised Dr. DuBois' Vietnam-era writing as dedicated to the advancement of knowledge, and that "throughout his professional life he had championed the cause of Africa in his writings, arguing for the recognition of the continent's contribution to world history" (Provenzo and Abaka 2012, 26).

It has been speculated that if Malcolm X had lived beyond 1965, he would have decided to take up citizenship in an African country, similar to what Dr. DuBois and others did, mainly because of his abhorrence of some of the foreign policy issues of the United States at the time. In fact, when Dr. DuBois died at the age of ninety-five on Tuesday, August 27, 1963, the announcement of his death included the details that he had gone to Accra, Ghana as a special guest of the late president Kwame Nkrumah as well as subsequently becoming director of the *Encyclopedia Africana* project, which was being sponsored by the Ghana government, and that he "became a citizen of Ghana this year [1963]" (Editor, *This Day,* August 28, 1963).

Dr. DuBois, who moved to Ghana in 1961, celebrated his ninety-first birthday in Peking (now Beijing), where he was honored with a birthday reception that was attended by Chou Enlai, the prime minister. It was, therefore, not surprising that Dr. DuBois, who also received the Lenin Peace Prize in Moscow in 1959, came out publicly against the American war against North Vietnam, which was also publicly opposed by Malcolm X, Dr. King, and other black leaders. It was over the war that, in 1963, Dr. DuBois criticized the heavy bombing of Vietnam and, as part of the protest, went to the American embassy in January to surrender his American passport and renounce his American citizenship. In return he became a Ghanaian citizen and received a Ghana passport. His protests in Ghana did not pass unnoticed as his other black compatriots in America, including Malcolm X, Dr. King, and others were also echoing similar protests.

For example, Malcolm X showed that he was not merely opposed to the Vietnam War—he used his usual wit during his public pronouncements to denounce the war. An illustration is when he gave a speech that came to be known as "The Ballot or the Bullet," in which he made it very clear that although the North Vietnamese were seen to be poor men and women with limited technology, their sheer fortitude and determination helped them to face foreign military might squarely.

Malcolm X, in fact, increased his anti-Vietnam War rhetoric toward the end of his life between 1964 and 1965. Interestingly, Dr. King toed a similar path for the year before he was assassinated; he used his public pronouncements to warn the United States of America about her actions. Like Malcolm X's ballot box speech, Dr. King gave his well-known speech titled "A Time to Break the Silence," at the historic Riverside Church on April 4, 1967, exactly one month before his assassination. It was a three-pronged speech that warned against American racist as well as materialistic and militaristic ways of life. It was interesting that it was not only in America that African-American leaders like Malcolm X and Dr. King were speaking out openly against the war. For, as underscored above, on the African continent, ninety-five-year-old Dr. DuBois followed his public pronouncements with action by, indeed, going to the American embassy to renounce his citizenship and surrender his American passport—an act that pro-Vietnam critics saw as being too little too late because, at ninety-five years old, the legendary Dr. DuBois no longer needed the convenience of the U.S. passport to travel.

Similar to what was happening in some capitals of African countries, where radical regimes existed, America's bloody engagement in Vietnam had helped in launching an anti-war movement. In an unprecedented way, at her *alma mater* (Antioch College), Mrs. Coretta Scott King publicly condemned the Vietnam War several months before her husband (Dr. King) did. In fact, it was much later in the spring of 1965 that Dr. King openly launched public attacks on the Vietnam War, which he saw as being an immoral war. In public speeches in front of black audiences in particular, Dr. King sought an end to the war. Although he was the elected president of the SCLC, Dr. King's own SCLC board of directors openly rebuked and urged him to cease his public condemnation of the American role in the Vietnam War, as the board members were apprehensive that there could be reprisals from the government of president Lyndon B. Johnson, which had succeeded the friendlier administration of assassinated president John F. Kennedy. Malcolm X had, by early 1965, shown that he was also an uncompromising, anti-Vietnam War black leader. Together with Dr. King, they were being seen in 1965 as the defining figures of the diaspora-based black freedom movement. In fact, the February assassination of Malcolm X made Dr. King's family and aides very much concerned that if he did not watch out, he would also be killed. When, later that year, the Voting Rights Act of 1965 was passed, Johnson administration officials and critics of Dr. King wanted black civil rights leaders, led by Dr. King, to reach an accommodation with the American government, due to the passage of the act.

In evaluating Malcolm X today, it is also plausible to underscore that his views converged with those of other radical black groups, even after his death. For example, on January 6, 1966, the Student Nonviolent Coordinating Committee (SNCC)—led by Stokely Carmichael (later called Kwame Ture) and others—unabashedly made public pronouncements to condemn the Vietnam War as being racist as well as imperialist in all of its manifestations. Interestingly, Dr. King started to link the Vietnam War to his war against poverty. As several observers have noted, with apt economic insights, Dr. King spoke loudly about the need for the American government to devote billions of dollars to help bring about an end to poverty in the United States since it was one of the affluent countries in the West, adding that doing so would bring about what he, Dr. King, saw as economic justice. Although Malcolm X had less than a year to live, his predictions about seeking redress for his fellow blacks "by any means necessary" did materialize. An example of such predictions was that not very long after Dr. King, several SCLC leaders and other civil rights groups, like the Urban League, euphorically witnessed the signing of the 1964 Voting Rights Act. A black suburb of Watts exploded in August of that year, less than seven months after Malcolm X died.

Within the context of Malcolm X's predictions and even suspicions, it was police violence that set the black community in Watts on fire, when for not less than six days, the community burned with over two dozen people killed, and no fewer than one thousand badly hurt and needing medical attention or hospitalization. As assessed, there was more than thirty-five million dollars in property damage. Malcolm X, Dr. King, Whitney M. Young, Jr., and others were adjudged right in their respective calls for economic redemption for their fellow blacks living in impoverished neighborhoods of America. When a commission by California governor Pat Brown and headed by former Central Intelligence Agency director John McCone investigated the Watts riots , it re-echoed the calls by Dr. King and others for an infusion of billions of dollars in investment in the poor black communities of California and other places. The report pointed out that the main factors leading to the riots were poor living conditions as well as transparently poor conditions in black educational institutions as well as high unemployment.

Although Malcolm X and Dr. King were supposed to have differed in their tactics for the attainment of freedom for blacks and America's downtrodden populace, their critique of America in the context of racism and other shortcomings seemed to intertwine. As noted elsewhere, Malcolm X was killed not long after he had uttered some of his harshest criticisms of America. Dr. King's last sermon (delivered on Sunday April, 7, 1968, a day before his assassination) was in fact titled, "Why America May Go to Hell." Dr. King felt sad that his fellow blacks would not be able to celebrate America's bicentennial, adding boldly that the country's Declaration of Independence did not have any real meaning in the context of its implementation vis-a-vis black lives.

When observers look at Malcolm X retrospectively, they wonder how he would have felt about the election of Mr. Barack H. Obama as the forty-fourth president of the United States. To such observers, while the SCLC's Dr. King, Urban League's Young, CORE's James Farmer, and other civil rights cohorts achieved some of their laurels in America's South, Malcolm X, on the other hand, made his own mark in America's North. Ironically, above all, for Americans, these achievements converged in the attainment of the crucial 1965 Voting Rights Act. Malcolm X did not see the act come into fruition for he fell at the hands of the assassins' bullets. Dr. King followed in similar sad footsteps when, three years later, on April 4, 1968, he was also gunned down. Although the Urban League's strong leader, Whitney M. Young, Jr., was not killed by an assassin's bullet like NAACP's Mississippi field leader Medgar Evers, Malcolm,

King, and others, he met his death by drowning in Lagos, Nigeria on March 11, 1971, evoking much suspicion, similar to the assassinations of Malcolm, King, and other black (and even white) leaders.

While still looking at ways in which Malcolm X has been either remembered or immortalized, as part of an evaluation of his iconic life, one does not need to go further than the November 1992 Spike Lee film Malcolm X, which, in the words of analysts and critics, was the touchstone and epic movie event that made actor Denzel Washington an A-List-movie superstar as well as firming up his status as a real auteur with whom to reckon. The film's chronological path to America's movie theaters has a story of its own, and confirms the historic status of Malcolm X today. It is widely known that not long after Malcolm X's death, Hollywood became interested in adapting his story. Toward that end, James Baldwin, the distinguished black author, was known to have written a screenplay in 1968. However, the subject matter, coupled with the existing political climate in the ensuing years, prevented a Malcolm X movie from being seriously considered for production.

It is of historical importance to relate that, in the end, Norman Jewison, who was known to have successfully directed one of Sidney Poitier's greatest films, In the Heat of the Night, was brought on board to lead the cast for Malcolm X, with Denzel Washington, who had earlier co-starred in Jewison's A Soldier's Story. It is important also to point out that although Jewison was a very well-known and respected filmmaker, there was still widespread concern about such a white director bringing the life of a great black nationalist like Malcolm X to America's big screen. Sadly, Jewison stepped aside or, as Spike Lee described his exit, bowed out gracefully. Instead, Spike Lee was installed as the director by the producers of the film. Sadly, Spike Lee was also seen as a polarizing choice for some, as an anti-Spike Lee rally was held in Harlem, led by the late black radical poet, Amiri Baraka (formerly known as LeRoi Jones). Although many observers felt that, with his excellent training in film, Lee was an excellent choice to direct the production, Baraka and his supporters believed that their protests were to ensure that Malcolm X's life was not trashed to make middle-class blacks (or Negroes) sleep easier, which would be a real sad spectacle. Baraka wanted Eddie Murphy to direct the film, as he claimed that his films were much better. This only added to the controversies over which the life of this great leader has engendered.

For example, it was a known fact that Denzel Washington had previously portrayed Malcolm in an off-Broadway production, which had won critical acclaim, but there were some black leaders, again including Baraka, who objected to his being given the big screen role because, in their estimation, he lacked resemblance to the real-life icon. Yet, it was a fact that Washington, who is about six feet tall, did really bear a resemblance to Malcolm, although in life, Malcolm X was six feet four. These concerns were nipped in the bud because, as it turned out, the various complaints about Spike Lee as the director and Denzel Washington as a star, were indeed the least of the production's problems, more so as Spike Lee, with excellent credentials, sought to make a truly epic film, by including footages from the holy sites in Mecca that Malcolm visited as part of his Islamic pilgrimage.

There was a new hurdle, as Warner Brothers, the studio prepared to finance the movie, was only willing to commit to a budget of roughly thirty million dollars. When Lee began to go over the budget, there was a legitimate threat that creditors would shut down the entire production. Lee pointed out that the budget that was earmarked for Malcolm X was not adequate to ensure the film's success. So in desperation, Lee sought for donations from among African America's "Who's Who" rich and famous to save the film. As expected, Bill Cosby, Oprah Winfrey, Janet Jackson, and Prince agreed to help in keeping the production afloat. Some other African American entrepreneurs interested in preserving for posterity the image of Malcolm X, including Magic Johnson and Michael Jordan, also came on board. Happily, the movie returned to solvency and Spike Lee was able to complete the film which was released to American theaters on November 18, 1992. Malcolm X, the movie, performed very well at the box office, as it earned forty-eight million dollars in the United States of America alone, perhaps grossing more money overseas including his beloved Africa. In *The Washington Post*, a film critic described Malcolm X as the most universally appealing film that Spike Lee made, which should be seen with its engrossing mosaic of history as well as both myth and sheer conjecture. Malcolm X, who had been immortalized in varied ways, was named by Ebert as the best film of the year as well as one of the best films of the 1990s.

Most certainly, Attallah Shabazz said it best when she pointed to the fact that her late iconic dad was, on January 20, 1999, further immortalized when the United States Postal Service issued a special commemorative postal stamp to honor the memory of her father, an acknowledgment that, as Ms. Shabazz said, affirmed the integrity of the heart and the wisdom of Malcolm's philosophy as well as guarantee that the message of her assassinated father would endure. Solemnly, she wrote in a foreword to her dear father's published memoirs that she had promised her famous parents: "As their eldest, I have pledged time and again to care for their daughters, my younger sisters, in their memory, in their honor, and with their celestial guidance" (Malcolm X 1999).

The fascination with Malcolm X has been so phenomenal that fifty years after his death, he still has admirers defending him left and right. For example, when Manning Marable, as Columbia University professor and a very distinguished scholar, took not less than a decade to complete his 594-page tome, *Malcolm X: A Life of Reinvention*, published in 2011, admirers of Malcolm took time and pains to peruse the entire book. In the end, they disagreed with several statements in the book that, to them, either attempted to defame or undermine their hero, Malcolm X. In fact, their efforts at correcting misstated facts about Malcolm X included publishing an entire book, titled *A Life of Reinvention: Correcting Manning Marable's Malcolm X*. For this work, published in early 2015, there were over a dozen contributors to the book that was co-edited by Jared A. Ball and Todd Steven Burroughs. These pro-Malcolm writers concluded, in a variety of essays, that what Dr. Marable wrote, to say the least, was a second assassination of Malcolm X (Ball and Burroughs 2015). That probably seems to be too much of a stretch.

Since it is a legal truism in many civilized societies that repeating a defamation or a libel can easily make the repeater also liable in a court of law of those two offenses, we do not intend to dignify here any of the unproven allegations any other authors, including Professor Marable, have made against Malcolm X. However, we can ascertain that there have certainly been similar responses by Malcolm X admirers or followers to criticisms of Malcolm X.

In fact, pro-Malcolm X individuals have also gone to the extent of indicating that there are several best ways of understanding the ideas of their assassinated hero (Malcolm X) when it comes to violence. In this way, they are trying to show that it was due to misinformation and misunderstanding to claim that Malcolm X (who had accomplished much by 1964 when he visited the Middle East and Africa) was still a violent man and a racist until his death in 1965. Instead, these Malcolm adherents point to existing tapes as well as lecture notes and also a publication with the title of *The Last Year of Malcolm X: The Evolution of a Revolutionary* that was authored by George Breitman and published by the New York-based Merit Publishers two years after Malcolm's assassination, in 1967. To help interested persons, pro-Malcolm followers point to the extensive listing of books, pamphlets, and magazine articles on or by Malcolm X that correct the wrongly created image of their icon.

In fact, also pointed to as part of the fascinating way of correcting wrong information about Malcolm X, is that there is a bibliographic source and other materials available in various places, including from the pages of the publication known as *The Militant*, published between 1960 and 1965. Such publications, as pro-Malcolm X writers have underscored, persistently presented what they consider to be an accurate account of what Malcolm X had to say, and occasionally ran stories correcting the false impressions given out by other anti-Malcolm publications, including some major newspapers in the United States. For example, interested persons in search of similar truths about Malcolm X, as part of the ongoing fascination with Malcolm X, have been pointed to Pathfinder Press of New York as the primary source for printed speeches and writings of Malcolm X beyond his own autobiography, which he was assisted in writing by the famous *Roots* author, Alex Haley. As a credible source, Malcolm X admirers make sure to reiterate that this particular press also publishes important books about Malcolm X that every serious student of Malcolm X must rely on and be grateful for, as Pathfinder publications go a long way, in the opinion of the pro-Malcolm individuals, to help in preserving Malcolm's iconic image.

CHAPTER 6

MALCOLM X AND AFRICAN LEADERS

During his interactions with African dignitaries and their diplomats at the United Nations' headquarters in New York, it was very clear that there was a measure of affection between them. It was the same when Malcolm visited Africa and met African leaders and their top political leaders and operatives. Yet, it has been shown that when Malcolm X appealed to these same leaders to assist him and other African Americans in their quest to place grievances on the agenda of the United Nations and the Organization of African Unity or the OAU (now called the African Union or AU), it was not an easy task. Malcolm X showed a lot of frustration for not succeeding in his designs for the support of African leaders and their diplomats to back his plan "to present blacks' grievances to international bodies in hopes of global intervention" (Marable 2011, 337).

What was, however, astonishing was that in the midst of the failure to embarrass the United States government and its officials that way, his five-month stay in Africa in 1964 truly saw him as the honored guest of several leaders on the continent as well as being seen as a beloved fellow black. In the end, Malcolm X "failed to persuade, though not for any great flaw in his argument or [the] ebbing of his passion; his rhetoric simply could not overcome the cold logic of international politics" (Marable 2011, 361–362). As the record of his 1964 travels in Africa showed, Malcolm X arrived in the Egyptian capital of Cairo, where that year's annual OAU conference of African heads of state was taking place. He was in Egypt to serve as an official observer in his capacity as the founding president of Muslim Mosque, Inc. (MMI) and the Organization of Afro-American Unity. He had arrived to stay at the Semiramis Hotel in Cairo, from where he would attend deliberations of the OAU meetings (Assensoh and Alex-Assensoh 2014; Marable 2011).

With plans to appeal to the African leaders of the newly independent countries on the continent to condemn America on grounds of human rights violations against blacks of America, Malcolm X had written a memorandum for distribution at the OAU meeting that year. The gist of his memorandum was that racism in the United States of America "is the same that it is in South Africa" (Marable 2011, 361). To Malcolm X, the success of his plans to get the African leaders to do his bidding (notwithstanding strong American public relations efforts undermining Malcolm X's efforts) would mean that the African leaders at the annual OAU conference were displaying true Pan-Africanism or showing that they were ready to embrace Pan-African politics. He publicly exclaimed that his unrelenting prayer was that the African leaders, who had valiantly fought colonialism, imperialism, and even neo-colonialism—just as Ghana's Nkrumah, Tanzania's Nyerere and others were harping on in their writings at the time—were not going to fall victim to what he described as the dollars of America (Marable 2011).

Over the years, it has become very clear that Malcolm X was ahead of his time in his strenuous efforts on behalf of his fellow African Americans against their adopted country, as several of them considered Africa as the original home of their ancestors. Although it was in the early 1960s that Malcom X was appealing to African leaders to issue a condemnation of America for human rights violations, it was not until June 27, 1981, that the Organization of African Unity (OAU), now the African Union, instituted its African Charter on Human and Peoples' Rights. In *Human Rights and the Environment: Cases, Law, And Policy* (2008), University of Oregon School of Law Professors Kravchenko and Bonine have provided an extensive discussion of the charter, which has provisions for several laudable measures. The two authors, in their book, have highlighted selected topical articles prominent in the charter. For example, article 16 sections 1 and 2 stress the fact that "Every individual shall have the right to enjoy the best attainable state of physical and mental health"; and that "State Parties in the present Charter shall take the necessary measures to protect the health of their people and to ensure that they receive medical attention when they are sick" (Kravchenko and Bonine 2008, 53).

In line with Malcolm X's wishes, it would have been ideal if the charter had been in place because, as further demonstrated in the 2008 book by Professors Kravchenko and Bonine, article 30, *inter alia*, read: "An African Commission on Human and People's Rights, hereinafter called "the Commission", shall be established within the organization of African unity [now the African Union] to promote human and Peoples' Rights and ensure their protection in Africa" (Kravchenko and Bonine 2008, 53).

As can be seen clearly, the continental Organization of Africa (OAU) did not have the foregoing provisions as part of its founding charter, which was signed in Addis Ababa, Ethiopia, on May 25, 1963. Even with the establishment of the 1963 charter, the organization (African Union) has as its main focus the struggle for the unification of the African continent, a major preoccupation of such radical African leaders as Ghana's Kwame Nkrumah, Guinea's Sekou Toure, Tanzania's Julius K. Nyerere, Uganda's Milton A. Obote, Egypt's Gamal Abdel Nasser, Kenya's Jomo Kenyatta, Zambia's Kenneth Kaunda, and several others.

In view of the foregoing, the agenda that Malcolm X brought to the 1964 OAU annual conference of the African leaders was at variance with what could be tabled as part of the discussions for that year. In Malcolm's view, his fellow African Americans living in such southern states of

America as Mississippi and Louisiana, respectively, faced environmental hazards, whereby their homes were close to polluting factories and other hazardous wastes. That, in his opinion, violated their human rights. It was, therefore, not only the OAU that Malcolm X approached, as he also went to the United Nations with his appeal.

For example, when it became apparent that the newly elected prime minister Patrice Lumumba of the Congo (now the Democratic Republic of the Congo (DRC)) had been murdered on January 17, 1961, allegedly by Belgian mercenaries back in the Congo, worldwide demonstrations were triggered in solidarity with Lumumba's forces, family, and friends throughout the world. Malcolm X and several black leaders in America were at the forefront of these demonstrations. The late professor Marable of Columbia University has underscored in his 2011 book, *A Life of Reinvention: Malcolm X*, that there was a coalition of divergent groups that, on February 15, 1961, demonstrated at the United Nations against the assassination of Lumumba. Apart from Malcolm and his male friends, there was his good friend, the late Maya Angelou, whose Cultural Association for Women of African Heritage, actively involved itself in the radical demonstrations at the United Nations' headquarters. Interestingly, as part of cold war politics, the United States government saw these demonstrations as being inspired by communist forces, thus making it seem as if the leaders, including Malcolm X and Angelou, were communist elements (Assensoh and Alex-Assensoh 2014; Marable 2011).

After the United Nations' event, to protest the assassination of Congolese prime minister Patrice Lumumba, Malcolm X still had plans to go before the world body in a different capacity. Since his Muslim Mosque, Inc. was geared toward the recruitment and training of black youth for Islam, he did not want to use it as a conduit to lodge a protest that he had in mind on behalf of his fellow blacks. Therefore, he decided in May 1964 that he would launch a new organization for political purposes. With trusted friends like Lynne Shifflett and Peter Bailey, plans were afoot for the launching of the organization of Afro-American Unity (OAAAU) to be headquartered in New York, possibly in his beloved Harlem (Assensoh and Alex-Assensoh 2014; Marable, 2011).

Still ahead of his time, Malcolm X's main aim was to launch the OAAU and, soon after, facilitate the interest of his fellow African Americans. Therefore, as Professor Marable disclosed in his 2011 book, Malcolm made it a number one priority to use the OAAU, as a new group, to present a case of his fellow blacks at the United Nations, where he would present several grievances to the world body on behalf of African Americans, whose human rights were, in his opinion, being denied by the government of the United States. He was doing so, according to Marable, "in hopes of seeking global intervention" (Marable 2011, 337; Assensoh and Alex-Assensoh 2014; 71).

What is interesting, at this stage, was the fact that it was too early in 1964 for Malcolm X to think about bringing human rights' violations against African Americans to the United Nations; hence many people felt that he was ahead of his time. For it was not until 1966 that the United Nations and its leadership would start to institute what has come to be known as the International Covenant on Civil and Political Rights, as documented in Professors Kravchenko's and Bonine's book, *Human Rights and the Environment: Cases, Law and Policy* (2008).

Although the covenant was debated, structured, and restructured earlier by the United Nations and its constituent units, the UN's International Covenant on Civil and Political Rights, in the words of Professors Kravchenko and Bonine, "entered into force in 1976"; with one hundred and sixty countries agreeing to be parties to the covenant, it is enforced by the Human Rights Committee of the United Nations (Kravchenko and Bonine 2008, 149).

If alive in 1976, perhaps Malcolm X would have gone to the United Nations to present his human rights' violation allegations against the United States, which happens to be a powerful member of the organization. It would have been an interesting spectacle were Malcolm to expect the

United Nations to take any measures against its host country, the United States, on whose soil the headquarters is situated in New York.

In retrospect, at that point, it would not have been impossible to have a United Nations' body to handle Malcolm X's complaints, especially since the new covenant of the U.N. was having its articles enforced by the Human Rights Committee, which was distinct from the former U.N. Commission on Human Rights or the present-day Human Rights Council. Instead, as Professors Kravchenko and Bonine have aptly underscored, the committee is made up of no fewer than eighteen experts, who meet three times a year to review compliance with the covenant. Interestingly, Professors Kravchenko and Bonine explained clearly that complaints that come before the United Nations' body are called "communications," while the complainants are known as "authors," but the results of the committee, upon its completion or disposition of complaints, are called "views" but, interestingly, not "verdicts."

Probably, Malcolm X's complaints against the United States would have fallen under article 27 of the United Nation's covenant, whereby it is categorically stated: "In those states in which ethnic, religious or linguistics minorities exist, persons belonging to such minorities shall not be denied the right, in community with the other members of their group, to enjoy their own culture, to profess and practice their own religion, or to use their own language." (Kravchenko and Bonine 2008, 149).

One wonders under which claims Malcolm would have chosen to lodge a complaint against the United States. However, there was a precedent, as disclosed in the book by Professors Kravchenko and Bonine, that the United Nations' committee has considered various complaints by indigenous people from elsewhere, who alleged that harm had been caused to their environment under article 27 of the United Nations' Covenant on Civil and Political Rights, but that most of the complaints have been unsuccessful, while others have seen moderate success. The query is whether Malcolm X and his allies would have prevailed against the United States, from which the United Nations derived a lot of moral and monetary support. On the other hand, it is not impossible that the committee would have entertained a complaint of environmental indignation, as many African Americans in states such as Louisiana and Mississippi often felt that factories, which emitted carbon dioxide and other toxic fumes and hazardous wastes, have been situated near their homes without due care. That, indeed, would have been part of Malcolm X's complaints.

Unfortunately, Malcolm X did not live to be able to utilize the new United Nations' covenant that came into existence in 1976, basically eleven years after the black Muslim leader's assassination. Yet, his admirers cherish the fact that he lived ahead of his time by trying to take measures in 1964 for which both the United Nations and the Organization of African Unity (OAU), now the African Union (AU), did not have the mandate to invoke. That, sadly, accounted for the reason that the two organizations and their leaders did not, in his day in the mid-1960s, entertain Malcolm X's loud complaints for sanctions against the United States.

For example, the charter of the then Organization of African Unity, which was signed into force on May 25, 1963, in Addis Ababa, Ethiopia, had no provisions to guide the leadership, made up of African heads of state and governments, to table and discuss Malcolm's claims against the United States, a country that was considered friends by several African nations and their political leaders. So far, the OAU charter had thirty-three (XXXIII) articles or provisions, all of which were numbered in Roman numerals (I-XXXIII). Of course, perusing the document, Malcolm X saw instances or traces of the mention of certain laudable phrases, which referred to African nations and their interconnectedness but not in relationship with countries based outside the continent of Africa.

What Malcolm X either forgot or was not aware of was the fact that even for African nations and their citizens, it was often a problem for the OAU leadership to take steps to sanction members of the organization because of a clause emphasizing non-interference in the internal affairs of member nations. Specifically, Article III of the Charter, *inter alia*, underscores in sections or principles 1 and 2 that there would be an adherence to the sovereign equality of all OAU member nations as well as "non-interference in the internal affairs of States" (Assensoh 1998, 161).

For example, the OAU Charter did specify under rights and duties of member nations that, as enshrined in Article V, "all member States [or Nations] shall enjoy equal rights and have equal duties," as pointed out in the book, *African Political Leadership* (Assensoh 1998). Yet that did not extend to blacks living in the United States, with whom Malcolm X was referencing as not having human and other rights, and that he should be supported in his quest for either public rebuke or sanctions against American political leaders that he considered to be the culprit. Apart from his fruitless appeals to the OAU annual conference in Cairo on behalf of his fellow African Americans, Malcolm X was quoted by Professor Marable in his seminal 2011 book that he wrote a letter to his wife (Betty) in the United States dated August 4, 1964, and mailed from the Egyptian capital, Cairo, in which he asked his wife to urge certain friends and also members of his organizations back home to cooperate in helping "to bring racial issue before the United Nations" (Marable 2011, 362). By that, the OAAU leader (Malcolm X) was referring to his complaints that he and his fellow blacks faced racism and unequal treatment in the United States. However, he did not realize that both the OAU and the UN did not have the legal instrument to deal with the issues that he was referring to, including racism.

Therefore, in retrospect, Malcolm X's admirers—who included his family members and many members of his Muslim Mosque, Inc., the Organization of Afro-American Unity, and, indeed, scholars studying his life and times—very strongly felt, and rightly so, that this black Muslim leader, who had by 1964 had left the Nation of Islam (NOI), was certainly ahead of his time, as he sought to utilize the OAU and the United Nations to seek relief for his fellow blacks. His legacy, therefore, has included being seen as a visionary leader, who knew what was good for his kith and kin (or other blacks). His oldest daughter, Attallah Shabazz, was right in her concluding words in the foreword to *The Autobiography of Malcolm X* when, among other details, she concluded: "Some [people] have said that my father was ahead of his time, but the truth is he was on time and perhaps we were late" (Malcolm X 1999, xxiv).

In fact, in February 2015, several public events were planned—together with television programs with appearances by Malcolm's daughter and experts—to commemorate the fiftieth anniversary of Malcolm X's assassination in the Audubon Theater Ballroom, where he was addressing an event organized by one of his two organizations, the Muslim Mosque, Inc. (MMI) and the Organization of Afro-American Unity (OAAU). There were seminars and conference panels planned to coincide with the anniversary. At the University of Oregon, for example, the local National Association for the Advancement of Colored People (NAACP) held its own commemorative event at the Many Nations Long House, which comes under the portfolio of the Division of Equity and Inclusion (DEI), headed by the university's vice-president for equity and inclusion and political science professor Yvette Marie Alex-Assensoh, who is the co-author of this book. Since we have published an earlier biography of Malcolm X, we were invited to speak about him and our book. We did point out that we were working on this book, which is much different from the biography because in this second Malcolm X publication, we were endeavoring to sow his closeness to the continent of Africa and how, for over four months, Malcolm X chose in 1964 to live in Africa, where he was warmly welcomed by African leaders, scholars, and ordinary citizens. According to some of the African citizens and scholars he interacted with, Malcolm X had plans to move his family eventually to the continent, which several civil rights leaders of the United States, including Rev. Dr. Martin Luther King, Jr., and the Rev. Jesse Jackson, Sr., referred to as the motherland.

Whether Malcolm X, his wife (Betty), and their entire family would have moved to live in Africa remained to be seen, although it was not impossible because he was impressed with the fact that wherever he went on the continent, black people were in leadership positions. That, indeed, was the new and independent Africa. In fact, several of his admirers were sad that Malcolm X did not act proactively by swiftly moving away from the United States, where he was earmarked for assassination.

Although Malcolm X was not stationed in one country for the many months that he stayed in Africa between June and August 1964, he still had the opportunity to sample the various cultural nuances and cuisines of the places he visited during that sojourn. According to individuals whom he spoke with, including African diplomats at the United Nations, Malcolm X was determined to move back to the continent in order to make sure that his entire family would experience the African hospitality that he felt everywhere. Above all, he also wanted his children to be raised with African and Pan-African awareness.

Sometimes, the query has been raised whether Malcolm X would have decided where to live in Africa based on religious, geographic, or cultural preferences. Some observers are, in retrospect, of the view that Malcolm would have settled down in a largely Islamic country like Egypt. In terms of West Africa, he did identify well with African American residents of Ghana, who had been attracted there by the late president Kwame Nkrumah. It was still felt that because of the humid weather, as a trans-Saharan terrain, it would not have been an ideal place for him.

Some Africans from East Africa thought that Malcolm X felt so much at home with late nationalist leaders like Tom Mboya of Kenya and Abdulrahman Muhammad Babu of Tanzania that the African American radical leader (Malcolm) would have chosen to live in either Kenya or Tanzania with his family. In either of the two places, he seemed happy with the leadership. Through Mboya and Babu, he had the opportunity to meet and interact very well with Kenyan and Tanzanian leaders. It was, for example, revealed that he sat in the midst of the late Kenyan president Jomo Kenyatta to sip tea, indeed together with several Kenyan cabinet members.

In Tanzania, Malcolm had the privilege of travelling with Babu to the Island of Zanzibar, his own home region from where he rose through the political ranks to become an important cabinet member, during which time he headed very crucial departments of the earlier government of the late president Julius K. Nyerere. Babu, for example, was a staunch Muslim and, as a result, Malcolm would have found it very convenient to live not far from him. Unfortunately, all of these were speculations, as Malcolm returned to the United States in the fall of 1964 to join his pregnant wife (Betty), who was expecting their twins and, without any concrete plans towards moving the family to Africa, he was to be assassinated a few months later in February 1965.

AMBASSADOR ALEX QUAISON-SACKEY'S ASSESSMENT OF MALCOLM X

Born in the former Gold Coast (now Ghana since 1957) on August 9, 1924, Dr. Alex Quaison-Sackey was barely a year older than Malcolm X (who was born in the United States on May 19,1925) when they first met at the United Nations, where Quaison-Sackey was Ghana's ambassador and permanent representative from June 1959 until he was appointed Ghana's foreign minister in Ghana in 1965. Unfortunately, his foreign ministry position was short lived because a few months after his appointment, the government of the late president Kwame Nkrumah was overthrown in a *coup d'etat* on February 24, 1966. Being very close to Nkrumah, he was in fact part of the Ghanaian leader's entourage to Southeast Asia when the *coup* took place and, as a result, he was dismissed by the military regime of the National Liberation Council (NLC).

At the time that Ambassador Quaison-Sackey was serving at the United Nations as well as being concurrent ambassador to Mexico and Cuba, Malcolm X was still an active member of the Nation of Islam (NOI). In fact, according to an interview with Ambassador Quaison-Sackey, their most substantive chance meeting took place on January 18, 1961, when Malcolm led several black Muslims to go to the United Nations to protest the assassination of Congolese prime minister Patrice Lumumba and two of his political allies.

According to the Ghanaian ambassador, he personally reported in a diplomatic dispatch to President Nkrumah's office, the impressive way Malcolm X had led the protest against Lumumba's assassination. Therefore, when Malcolm's third child (Ilysah) was born in July 1962, he (Quaison-Sackey) brought a monetary gift for Malcolm and Betty for them to buy a gift for the baby. From that time on, they became fast friends and, as a result, when Malcolm wanted to visit Ghana as well as to attend then Organization of African Unity (OAU) events, the Ghana ambassador facilitated that interest for Malcolm.

From 1964 to 1972, Guinea's Diallo Boubacar Telli left his country's United Nations ambassadorial position to become the first secretary-general of the OAU, with its headquarters at Addis Ababa, Ethiopia. Since Guinea and Ghana were very close, Ambassadors Telli and Quaison-Sackey were very close diplomatic friends. Apart from Ambassador Quaison-Sackey exchanging ideas with Guinea's U.N. Ambassador Telli and also holding long conversations, the Ghanaian diplomat "developed a personal friendship with Malcolm X" (Jenkins and Tryman, 2002, 455). In fact, when Malcolm X asked for help to be credentialed so that he could represent the Organization of Afro-American Unity (OAAU) at the 1964 OAU annual conference in Cairo, Egypt, the Ghanaian ambassador made that happen easily; hence Malcolm wore an official badge as an observer at the July 1964 OAU heads of state meeting (Assensoh and Alex-Assensoh 2014).

In fact, a year before former Ambassador Quaison-Sackey's death on December 21, 1992, at Ghana's Korle Bu Hospital of pulmonary embolism, there was an opportunity to speak with him again about Malcolm X, thanks to former Ghana United Nations ambassador Kofi N. Awoonor, who facilitated this meeting in Accra. Interestingly, he still remembered him very well. After explaining that Dr. Quaison-Sackey was not in the best of health, the agreement was to have a brief conversation to clarify a point from a previous discussion. When he knew it was about Malcolm X, he opened up.

Former Ambassador Quaison-Sackey lamented the fact that when the Supreme Military Council II (SMC II) leader, the late lieutenant general Fred Akuffo appointed him Ghana's ambassador to the United States in 1978, he had plans to visit the Schomburg Center for Research in Black Culture in Harlem, where he knew that Malcolm X's papers were deposited. He was interested in doing research to write his memoirs, in which his relationship with Malcolm X would have played a major part in the discussions about his ambassadorial duties at the United Nations in particular and the United States in general.

Dr. Quaison-Sackey did remember that he had written an earlier book, which was too early to capture all of those historic moments. His earlier book was *Africa Unbound: Reflections of an African Statesman*, which was published in May 1963 by Praeger. He was happy that, at least, he was able to describe his understanding of Senegalese president Leopold S. Senghor's concept of Negritude, which he had described as the total acceptance and re-affirmation of blackness in general; in view of his strong African nationalist as well as diplomatic credentials and close friendship with Malcolm X, it was not surprising that he was described as "a fiery opponent of colonialism, racism, and apartheid and a staunch Pan-Africanist," (Jenkins and Tryman, 2002, 455).

Sadly for Ambassador Quaison-Sackey, the military regime of General Akuffo was overthrown in a *coup d'etat* led by then flight lieutenant Jerry John Rawlings of the Ghana Air Force, who instituted his Armed Forces Revolutionary Council (AFRC), which meant that Dr. Quaison-Sackey was relieved of his position as the representative of the overthrown government. That also meant his plans to write about Malcolm X was not to happen. Therefore, in the last interview, former Ambassador Quaison-Sackey wanted to place on record that Malcolm X was a very trustworthy friend, who lived a dignified life. He was, therefore, sorry that the black Muslim leader's detractors often tried to use his earlier police arrests as a yardstick to measure his entire life. To him, they were childhood indiscretions.

In fact, as part of an interview, Dr. Quaison-Sackey said that he knew that sometimes Malcolm X and his wife (Betty) had financial problems. Yet, he also felt that Malcolm did not allow that to overshadow his daily existence. It was at that point that he mentioned an interesting scenario that took place at the private quarters of the Ghana mission to the United Nations. He mentioned how he had a meeting with Malcolm X on the second floor of the building and had a light lunch with him. He (Dr. Quaison-Sackey) went to the restroom, and when he came back Malcolm handed to him an envelope that fell out of his pocket. It contained $1,500, which was the money meant to pay, in cash, for a major plumbing repair job carried out by a young plumber, who did not accept a payment in checks (cheques).

"Brother Ambassador, you dropped this envelope," said Malcolm, as he handed the envelope back to him with the entire money in it intact. "That was honesty beyond anything else," ex-Ambassador Quaison-Sackey said about Malcolm X, adding that such a noble act on Malcolm's part made him (the former Ambassador) sad when he heard his critiques alluding to his childhood arrests or imprisonment.

As we researched the life and times of Malcolm X, we very often wished that publishers would not include in our publications about Malcolm X any of the early photos of his life and captions about his police arrests or imprisonment. However, we have no control over such matters, but we are happy that we can point out some of the positive things that have been said about this black icon, especially as his death is being remembered some fifty years since his passing.

Also, it would have been great if former Ambassador Quaison-Sackey was able to write his own second memoirs, in which he would have paid tribute to the positive legacy of Malcolm X, who was described by Actor Ossie Davis in his eulogy as a shining black prince; the same Davis looked at how John Brown's abolitionist activities were earlier deemed to be treasonable, but he was later embraced as a black hero but not a traitor. The famous actor added that he would not be surprised if men and women came to see Malcolm X, in his own way and inimitable style, "also as a martyr in that cause" (Malcolm X 1999; 466).

APPENDIX

CHARTER OF THE ORGANIZATION OF AFRICAN UNITY

We, the Heads of African States and Governments assembled in the City of Addis Ababa, Ethiopia;

CONVINCED that it is the inalienable right of all people to control their own destiny;

CONSCIOUS of the fact that freedom, equality, justice and dignity are essential objectives for the achievement of the legitimate aspirations of the African peoples;

CONSCIOUS of our responsibility to harness the natural and human resources of our continent for the total advancement of our peoples in all spheres of human endeavour;

INSPIRED by a common determination to promote understanding among our peoples and co-operation among our States in response to the aspirations of our peoples for brother-hood and solidarity, in a larger unity transcending ethnic and national differences;

CONVINCED that, in order to translate this determination into a dynamic force in the cause of human progress, conditions for peace and security must be established and maintained;

DETERMINED to safeguard and consolidate the hard-won independence as well as the sovereignty and territorial integrity of our States, and to fight against neo-colonialism in all its forms;

DEDICATED to the general progress of Africa;

PERSUADED that the Charter of the United Nations and the Universal Declaration of Human Rights, to the Principles of which we reaffirm our adherence, provide a solid foundation for peaceful and positive co-operation among States;

DESIROUS that all African States should henceforth unite so that the welfare and well-being of their peoples can be assured;

RESOLVED to reinforce the links between our states by establishing and strengthening common institutions;

HAVE agreed to the present Charter.

ESTABLISHMENT

Article I

1. The High Contracting Parties do by the present Charter establish an organization to be known as the **ORGANIZATION OF AFRICAN UNITY**. The Organization shall include the Continental African States, Madagascar and other Islands surrounding Africa.

PURPOSES
Article II

1. The Organization shall have the following purposes:

1. to promote the unity and solidarity of the African States;
2. to co-ordinate and intensify their co-operation and efforts to achieve a better life for the peoples of Africa;
3. to defend their sovereignty, their territorial integrity and independence;
4. to eradicate all forms of colonialism from Africa; and
5. to promote international co-operation, having due regard to the Charter of the United Nations and the Universal Declaration of Human Rights.

2. To these ends, the Member States shall co-ordinate and harmonize their general policies, especially in the following fields:

1. political and diplomatic co-operation;
2. economic co-operation, including transport and communications;
3. educational and cultural co-operation;
4. health, sanitation, and nutritional co-operation;
5. scientific and technical co-operation; and
6. co-operation for defense and security.

PRINCIPLES
Article III

The Member States, in pursuit of the purposes stated in Article II, solemnly affirm and declare their adherence to the following principles:

1. the sovereign equality of all Member States;
2. non-interference in the internal affairs of States;
3. respect for the sovereignty and territorial integrity of each State and for its inalienable right to independent existence;
4. peaceful settlement of disputes by negotiation, mediation, conciliation or arbitration;
5. unreserved condemnation, in all its forms, of political assassination as well as of subversive activities on the part of neighboring States or any other States;
6. absolute dedication to the total emancipation of the African territories which are still dependent;
7. affirmation of a policy of non-alignment with regard to all blocs.

MEMBERSHIP
Article IV

Each independent sovereign African State shall be entitled to become a Member of the Organization.

RIGHTS AND DUTIES OF MEMBER STATES

Article V

All Member States shall enjoy equal rights and have equal duties.

Article VI

The Member States pledge themselves to observe scrupulously the principles enumerated in Article III of the present Charter.

INSTITUTIONS
Article VII

The Organization shall accomplish its purposes through the following principal institutions:

1. the Assembly of Heads of State and Government;
2. the Council of Ministers;
3. the General Secretariat;
4. the Commission of Mediation, Conciliation and Arbitration.

THE ASSEMBLY OF HEADS OF STATE AND GOVERNMENT

Article VIII

The Assembly of Heads of State and Government shall be the supreme organ of the Organization. It shall, subject to the provision of this Charter, discuss matters of common concern to Africa with a view to co-ordinating and harmonizing the general policy of the Organization. It may in addition review the structure, functions and acts of all the organs and any specialized agencies which may be created in accordance with the present Charter.

Article IX

The Assembly shall be composed of the Heads of State and Government or their duly accredited representatives and it shall meet at least once a year. At the request of any Member State and on approval by a two-thirds majority of the Member States, the Assembly shall meet in extraordinary session.

Article X

1. Each Member State shall have one vote.
2. All resolutions shall be determined by a two-thirds majority of the Members of the Organization.
3. Questions of procedure shall require a simple majority. Whether or not a question is one of procedure shall be determined by a simple majority of all Member States of the Organization.
4. Two-thirds of the total membership of the Organization shall form a quorum at any meeting of the Assembly.

Article XI

The Assembly shall have the power to determine its own rules of procedure.

THE COUNCIL OF MINISTERS

Article XII

1. The Council of Ministers shall consist of Foreign Ministers or such other ministers as are designated by the Governments of Member States.
2. The Council of Ministers shall meet at least twice a year. When requested by any Member State and approved by two-thirds of all Member States, it shall meet in extraordinary session.

Article XIII

1. The Council of Ministers shall be responsible to the Assembly of Heads of State and Government. It shall be entrusted with the responsibility of preparing conferences of the Assembly.

2. It shall take cognizance of any matter referred to by the Assembly. It shall be entrusted with the implementation of the decision of the Assembly of Heads of State and Government. It shall co-ordinate inter-African co-operation in accordance with the instructions of the Assembly and in conformity with Article II [2] of the present Charter.

Article XIV

1. Each Member State shall have one vote.

2. All resolutions shall be determined by a simple majority of the members of the Council of Ministers.

3. Two-thirds of the total membership of the Council of Ministers shall form a quorum for any meeting of the Council.

Article XV

The Council shall have the power to
determine its own rules of procedure.

GENERAL SECRETARIAT
Article XVI

There shall be a Secretary General of the Organization, who shall be appointed by the Assembly of Heads of State and Government. The Secretary General shall direct the affairs of the Secretariat.

Article XVII

There shall be one or more Assistant Secretaries General of the. Organization, who shall be appointed by the Assembly of Heads of State and Government.

Article XVIII

The functions and conditions of service of the Secretary General, of the Assistant Secretaries General and other employees of the Secretariat shall be governed by the provisions of this Charter and the regulations approved by the Assembly of Heads of State and Government.

1. In the performance of their duties the Secretary General and the staff shall not seek or receive instructions from any government or from any other authority external to the Organization. They shall refrain from any action which might reflect on their position as international officials responsible only to the Organization.
2. Each member of the Organization undertakes to respect the exclusive character of the responsibilities of the Secretary General and the staff and not to seek to influence them in the discharge of their responsibilities.

COMMISSION OF MEDIATION CONCILIATION AD ARBITRATION

Article XIX

Member States pledge to settle all disputes among themselves by peaceful means and, to this end decide to establish a Commission of Mediation, Conciliation and Arbitration, the composition of which and conditions of service shall be defined by a separate Protocol to be approved by the Assembly of Heads of State and Government. Said Protocol shall be regarded as forming an integral part of the present Charter.

SPECIALIZED COMMISSION
Article XX

The Assembly shall establish such Specialized Commissions as it may deem necessary, including the following:

1. Economic and Social Commission;
2. Educational, Scientific, Cultural and Health Commission;
3. Defense Commission.

Article XXI

Each Specialized Commission referred to in Article XX shall be composed of the Ministers concerned or other Ministers or Plenipotentiaries designated by the Governments of the Member States.

Article XXII

The functions of the Specialized Commissions shall be carried out in accordance with the provisions of the present Charter and of the regulations approved by the Council of Ministers.

THE BUDGET

Article XXIII

The budget of the Organization prepared by the Secretary General shall be approved by the Council of Ministers. The budget shall be provided by contribution from Member States in accordance with the scale of assessment of the United Nations; provided, however, that no Member State shall be assessed an amount exceeding twenty percent of the yearly regular budget of the Organization. The Member States agree to pay their respective contributions regularly.

SIGNATURE AND RATIFICATION OF CHARTER
Article XXIV

1. This Charter shall be open for signature to all independent sovereign African States and shall be ratified by the signatory States in accordance with their respective constitutional processes.

2. The original instrument, done, if possible in African languages, in English and French, all texts being equally authentic, shall be deposited with the Government of Ethiopia which shall transmit certified copies thereof to all independent sovereign African States.

3. Instruments of ratification shall be deposited with the Government of Ethiopia, which shall notify all signatories of each such deposit.

ENTRY INTO FORCE
Article XXV

This Charter shall enter into force immediately upon receipt by the Government of Ethiopia of the instruments of ratification from two-thirds of the signatory States.

REGISTRATION OF THE CHARTER
Article XXVI

This Charter shall, after due ratification, be registered with the Secretariat of the United Nations through the Government of Ethiopia in conformity with Article 102 of the Charter of the United Nations.

INTERPRETATION OF THE CHARTER
Article XXVII

Any question which may arise concerning the interpretation of this Charter shall be decided by a vote of two-thirds of the Assembly of Heads of State and Government of the Organization.

ADHESION AND ACCESSION
Article XXVIII

1. Any independent sovereign African State may at any time notify the Secretary General of its intention to adhere or accede to this Charter.

2. The Secretary General shall, on receipt of such notification, communicate a copy of it to all the Member States. Admission shall be decided by a simple majority of the Member States. The decision of each Member State shall be transmitted to the Secretary General,

3. who shall, upon receipt of the required number of votes, communicate the decision to the State concerned.

MISCELLANEOUS
Article XXIX

The working languages of the Organization and all its institutions shall be, if possible African languages, English and French.

Article XXX

The Secretary General may accept, on behalf of the Organization, gifts, bequests and other donations made to the Organization, provided that this is approved by the Council of Ministers.

Article XXXI

The Council of Ministers shall decide on the privileges and immunities to be accorded to the personnel of the Secretariat in the respective territories of the Member States.

CESSATION OF MEMBERSHIP
Article XXXII

Any State which desires to renounce its membership shall forward a written notification to the Secretary General. At the end of one year from the date of such notification, if not withdrawn, the Charter shall cease to apply with respect to the renouncing State, which shall thereby cease to belong to the Organization.

AMENDMENT OF THE CHARTER
Article XXXIII

This Charter may be amended or revised if any Member State makes a written request to the Secretary General to that effect; provided, however, that the proposed amendment is not submitted to the Assembly for consideration until all the Member States have been duly notified of it and a period of one year has elapsed. Such an amendment shall not be effective unless approved by at least two-thirds of all the Member States.

IN FAITH WHEREOF, We, the Heads of African States and Governments have signed this Charter.

shall not be effective unless approved by at least two-thirds of all the Member States.

IN FAITH WHEREOF, We, the Heads of African States and Governments have signed this Charter.

Done in the City of Addis-Ababa, Ethiopia, this 25th day of May, 1963.

Member Nations of the OAU

Figure 1. Member nations of the OAU

Algeria	Equatorial Guinea	Malawi	Sierra Leone
Angola	Ethiopia	Mali	Somalia
Benin	Gabon	Mauritania	South Africa
Botswana	Gambia	Mauritius	Sudan
Burundi	Ghana	Morocco	Swaziland
Cameroon	Guinea	Mozambique	Tanzania
Cape Verde	Guinea-Bissau	Namibia	Togo
Central African Republic	Ivory Coast	Niger	Tunisia
Chad	Kenya	Nigeria	Uganda
Comoros	Lesotho	Rwanda	Upper Volta
Congo	Liberia	South Tome and Principe	Zaire
Djibouti	Libya	Senegal	Zambia
Egypt	Madagascar	Seychelles	Zimbabwe

Courtesy of the Headquarters of the OAU, Addis Ababa, Ethiopia.
Member nations when the OAU was renamed African Union.

Malcolm X, St. Clair Drake, and African-American Leaders in Ghana

Abstract

This brief study, thematically, addresses several aspects of the contributions of African American intellectuals as well as business men and women to Ghana under the leadership of the late President Kwame Nkrumah. Such black leaders in Ghana made sure of encouraging other African American leaders back home, including Malcolm X, Martin Luther King, Jr., and others, to visit the motherland, as Malcolm and several others referred to Ghana. The moving forces in the whole scenario were leading diaspora-based black scholars, who played leadership roles in those efforts. At the fountainhead was the late Professor St. Clair Drake of Stanford University (born and named John Gibbs St. Clair Drake), who has aptly been described above in flattery terms as a mainstream scholar and a public intellectual, who was very close to Malcolm X and other civil rights leaders. Drake's published 1945 sociological study, which made him famous, has stood the test of time and established him very early on as a scholar with whom to reckon. As the records have demonstrated, he influenced several of his intellectual colleagues to move with him to the new Ghana, which had then attained its independence from the United Kingdom and changed its name from the Gold Coast to that of the ancient empire name of Ghana on March 6, 1957. In doing so, Professor Drake and several of his intellectual colleagues, who mostly came at the time from Historically Black Colleges (HBCUs) went to impart their knowledge and expertise to the Ghanaian citizenry. They also saw how important spiritually and otherwise to attract Malcolm X, King, and others to African countries. This brief study for a conference at Berkeley, California, places emphasis on Dr. Drake, but we will also draw on facts from his relationship with Malcolm, King, and the others. Dr. Drake, for example, served as a full professor and also as Dean of Social Sciences at University of Ghana, which at the time in the 1960s was attaining its own identity but not as an appendage of University of London and other British universities. The study also underscores facts about several other intellectuals from the black diaspora, who teamed up with Professor Drake in those noble efforts. It is shown that it was in the spirit of Pan-Africanism that Ghana benefitted from all of the black leaders, who came to Ghana either for short- or long-term visits. At the top was Professor St. Clair Drake, who had befriended America-educated Kwame Nkrumah, Ghana's first elected indigenous head of state, whose indigenous title is Osagyefo. Dr. Drake and other black intellectuals from America teased him openly about this title. Above all, it will be shown, even if briefly, that Professor Drake—as social science faculty dean and St. Clair Drake of University of Ghana—played active roles in efforts to bring Malcolm X and several other "American Africans"—as Professor Gaines called them—to Ghana and made sure that they gave radical lectures on the university campus, just as Malcolm indeed did!

AFRICA AND THE ST. CLAIR DRAKE CONNECTION

The name of Professor St. Clair Drake invokes unlimited sentimental and historical memories when one considers the amount of intellectual progress that Ghana made in the 1960s because of the transparent contributions of several African Americans who moved to the West African nation, including Dr. Drake. He was one of several diaspora-based African Americans who heeded the June 1951 clarion call of the Prime Minister of the then Gold Coast Kwame Nkrumah, in which he invited African Americans (then called Negroes) to return to Ghana to help develop the country, which he and the diaspora-based black leaders referred to as the Negro's motherland and ancestral home. In his commencement speech at Lincoln University in Pennsylvania, Nkrumah also wanted such black leaders as Malcolm X, King, Dr. W.E.B. DuBois, and others to treat the then Gold Coast (which became Ghana in 1957) as a spiritual home like Mecca, which Muslims visit to perform their Haj.

In the speech, Nkrumah told his predominantly African American audience: "We are aiming to work under democratic-principles such as exist in Britain and in the United States," adding that his African nation (at the time called the Gold Coast because of its plentiful gold reserves) needed technicians, machinery, and capital to develop its natural resources, and added: "there was much for Negroes [now known as African Americans] to do to help their ancestral country." The historic context was that, six years before Ghana's independence in 1957, Dr. Kwame Nkrumah (who would become Ghana's first prime minister and president, respectively) visited the USA in his capacity as "Leader of Government Business" (a virtual prime minister) of the then Gold Coast, which was still under British colonial rule. Nkrumah was returning to Lincoln University in Pennsylvania, his alma mater, at the invitation of the university's president Horace Mann Bond, who conferred on Lincoln University's famous alumnus from Africa the honorary Doctor of Laws (LL.D) degree approved overwhelmingly by the university's Board of Trustees.

Nkrumah, a very good friend of Professor St. Clair Drake, Martin Luther King, and others, was an undergraduate student of Lincoln University, one of the oldest colleges of higher learning established in the 1800s for freed slaves. Nkrumah earned two academic degrees from Lincoln: a bachelor of arts degree in economics and sociology (1939); and a bachelor of theology degree (1942) from the Lincoln Theological Seminary (after which he went on to earn two master's degrees in education and philosophy from the nearby University of Pennsylvania. He completed the coursework for his doctoral degree in philosophy at the same university but, because of ill health, abandoned the quest for that degree and remained an ABD.

Paul Coffie, from New England, became the moving force behind the many freed slaves who chose to return to Africa by settling in Liberia in the 1830s. Professor Drake played a similar role in trying to rally his fellow black intellectuals for a similar Marcus Garvey-inspired "Return to Africa" movement. By the early 1960s, the migrating blacks from the United States were in an exodus to Ghana, either for short-term visits or long-term stays. It all began in March 1957 when the late Rev. Dr. Martin Luther King Jr. and his wife (Mrs. Coretta Scott King) paid their first and only joint visit to Ghana and, later, Nigeria as a result of Nkrumah's invitation. After the visit, Dr. King preached a sermon about the new Ghana titled "Birth of a New Nation" at the Dexter Avenue Baptist Church in Montgomery, Alabama. Mrs. King, too, wrote in admirable and historic terms about the 1957 trip in her 372-page memoirs, titled *My Life with Martin Luther King Jr.*, published in 1969 by Holt Rinehart and Winston.

When Professor Drake moved to Ghana, his immediate plan was to teach at University of Ghana at Legon, near the Ghanaian capital of Accra. Apart from being named a full professor, he was also appointed the Dean of the Faculty of Social Sciences. He and several African American intellectuals and professionals contributed immensely to Ghana's development from the intellectual and academic standpoint.

Some of the historic events and selected correspondence between the Kings, Drake, and other African Americans and Ghana's President Nkrumah have recently been documented in Volume VI of the Stanford University-based Martin Luther King Jr. Papers Project (on which both of us served in the 1990s: Professor A.B. Assensoh as Director of Research/ Associate Editor, and Professor Alex-Assensoh as a doctoral student at The Ohio State University in Columbus, Ohio.

According to the historic records, black men and women of the American diaspora who were encouraged by Professor Drake and others to answer Ghana President Nkrumah's call to visit or reside in Ghana between 1957 and 1960s were: A. Phillip Randolph, the trade unionist; then black Harlem Congressman Adam Clayton Powell; the Nobel Peace Prize winner and UN Under-Secretary-General Ralph Bunche; Lucille Armstrong (representing her husband, Louis Armstrong, the jazz legend); and university presidents Horace Mann Bond (Lincoln) and Mordecai

Johnson (Howard). Also visiting Ghana were Professor Lawrence Dunbar Reddick, who wrote *Crusader Without Violence*, an authorized biography of Rev. Dr. Martin Luther King, and a close friend of Dr. Nkrumah and Dr. Nnamdi Azikiwe of Nigeria; Julian and Ana Cordero Mayfield; W. Alphaeus Hunton; Roy Wilkins; Ras Makonnen of Guyana, who helped in organizing the 1945 Pan-African Congress in Manchester, UK, and later directed Nkrumah's African Affairs Bureau in Ghana; Michael Manley, the future radical prime minister of Jamaica; C.L.R. James, the Trinidadian radical scholar; and George Padmore (formerly called Malcolm Nurse), the great Caribbean-born Pan-Africanist. Dr. W.E.B. DuBois, the legendary black scholar, and his wife Mrs. Shirley Graham DuBois also moved to Ghana, where in February 1963, he celebrated his 95th birthday by taking up Ghanaian citizenship as part of his protest against the Vietnam War and the famous civil rights' march on Washington, DC. Dr. DuBois died in Ghana. He had been invited to go to Ghana earlier, but he could not make the trip because his American passport had, reportedly, been "withdrawn" by the State Department allegedly, on suspicion of being a communist sympathizer.

Other American professionals and scholars, who heeded Nkrumah's call to return home were Maya Angelou, the well-known author noted for her 1984 book on African children, *All God's Children Need Travelling Shoes*, and the acclaimed 1993 book, *The Heart of a Woman*; Leslie Alexander Lacy, author of the 1970 memoir of his Ghana years, *The Rise and Fall of a Proper Negro;* Alphaeus Hunton; Alice Windom; Wendell J. Pierre; Eric Eustace Williams, the Oxford-educated scholar and author of Capitalism and Slavery, who later became Prime Minister of Trinidad and Tobago; Neville Dawes, the famous Jamaican novelist; Frantz Fanon, the Martinique scholar, who was well known for such radical books as *Dying Colonialism* as well as *Wretched of the Earth, Black Skin White Mask;* and Sir W. Arthur Lewis, the West Indian Economist, who won the Nobel Economics Prize and also became an economic adviser to Ghanaian President Nkrumah. The motley crew included James Farmer, the civil rights leader; Muhammad Ali (the world's heavyweight boxing champion, then called Cassius Clay); Professor John Henrik Clarke, then of Hunter College (New York), whose papers—including his correspondence with Nkrumah—were donated to the New York Public Library's Schomburg Centre for Research in Black Culture.

With anthropological hindsight, Professor Drake often recalled—and was also confirmed by Mrs. Coretta Scott King—the fact that the black and white American connection to Ghana has very fascinating scenarios or anecdotes. An example, as Professor Drake and Mrs. King have confirmed at different occasions, it was at Ghana's independence celebratory event that Rev. Dr. and Mrs. King first met America's then vice-president, Richard Nixon, who was leading the official USA delegation to the Accra events. Not knowing who Dr. King was at the time. Mr. Nixon reportedly congratulated him on his country attaining its freedom. "No, I am not free yet. I am from Alabama. My name is Martin Luther King Jr." Dr. King reportedly told Nixon.

In heeding Nkrumah's call to return to Ghana, as an ancestral home, Professor St. Clair Drake and many diaspora-based blacks, including those from Caribbean nations, flocked to live and work in Ghana. Some other black leaders paid casual visits only. One of them was Malcolm X, who arrived in Ghana on May 10, 1964, on a pilgrimage-type of trip. Among blacks from the diaspora already in Ghana was Julian Mayfield and his wife. In fact, Mayfield headed a committee to welcome and shepherd Malcolm X to his speaking engagements in the Ghanaian capital of Accra.

University of Michigan history professor Kevin K. Gaines has thoroughly researched an aspect of these historic events, from which he authored his 342-page book, *American-Africans in Ghana: Black Expatriates and the Civil Rights Era* (published in 2006 by the University of North Carolina Press. In that book, it has been documented that, through the hard-working efforts of Professor Drake and Julian Mayfield, a well-known black writer, about three hundred African Americans agreed to move to Ghana, especially at the time that Professor Drake lived and worked there. They were, indeed, serving Ghana, as an ancestral country, in a variety of ways.

Professor Drake made it a point of often discussing how the African American presence in Ghana did help jumpstart several innovative projects. For example, the legendary Dr. W.E.B. DuBois began work on the historic Encyclopedia Africana project. Upon Dr. DuBois' death in 1963 (during the week of the black march on Washington led by Mr. King), Professor Ofosu-Appiah, a Ghanaian scholar who had understudied Dr. DuBois, took over the project as its new director but, due to financial difficulties, the project was suspended until Harvard University professor Henry Louis Gates Jr, and the Princeton University philosophy professor Kwame Anthony Appiah abridged and published their own impressive version of Microsoft's 1999 Encarta Africana Encyclopedia, considered a sequel to Dr. DuBois' project. Ghana's media and academic institutions benefited immensely from the expertise of these African-American scholars.

In *American-Africans in Ghana*, Gaines has confirmed the substantive role played by Dr. Drake and his intellectual cohorts, including placing an emphasis on the fact that "the story of the African American expatriate community in Nkrumah's Ghana illuminates the challenges and contradictions posed by Cold War liberalism and American hegemony during the 1960s. The American nation's declared support for desegregation, formal equality, and de-colonization masked the repression of black radicals."

In studying the life and times of Professor Drake, it comes out transparently that Ghana's late President Nkrumah, with his deep-rooted Pan-African and diaspora-based black interests, admired the serious promises of returning to Ghana made and kept in correspondence with USA-based blacks like Dr. Drake. That was the apparent reason for him to consider very seriously the return of African-Americans to Ghana. Very interestingly, when Dr. Drake and the late history professor Lawrence Dunbar Reddick introduced Richard Wright to the Ghanaian leader, he embraced him without hesitation as a brother from the black diaspora in the United States and also in France. The introduction was the main reason for Nkrumah, as an African leader, in the then Gold Coast, to write a letter of favorable attestation (styled "To Whom It May Concern") for Richard Wright, author of various classics, including the book, *Black Boy*. The historic introductory letter (which is published in his new book) was for Wright to obtain an entry visa to enter the then British-controlled Gold Coast to complete his research for his book manuscript, which was later published as *Black Power*.

Having been greatly impressed by the scholarship, literary acumen, and intellectual precision of such black scholars as Drake, Mayfield, Leslie Lacy, Maya Angelou, and others, Ghana's Nkrumah virtually regarded U.S.-based blacks as an extension of their African kith and kin. That was why he referred to the freedom of all black people in and outside Africa when—on the night that Ghana received her independence from the British authorities on March 6, 1957—he publicly declared as part of his independence oration that the independence of Ghana would "be meaningless unless it was linked up with the total liberation of Africa."

St. Clair Drake, Malcolm, King, and Others

Compared to Malcolm, King and the others, St. Clair Drake had the interest to move immediately to Africa, where he and his spouse would settle in Nkrumah's Gold Coast or, if after 1957, then Ghana. While Drake and his scholarly colleagues moved *en mass* to serve as faculty members, Malcolm, King, and the others only went for short visits, except for the 1964 extended visit of Malcolm X to several African countries for not less than four months. Many persons have wondered about St. Clair Drake who played such a pivotal role.

Therefore, in a write-up of a similar query-oriented title, Margot D. Weiss disclosed that, as mentioned earlier, Professor Drake was named, at birth, as John Gibbs St. Clair Drake. He has variously been described as a pioneering black social anthropologist as well as an activist, and that he was one of the nine known black anthropologists before World War II. His scholarship embodied ethnographic studies of race, social structure as well as class, with a lifelong quest for the eradication of social inequalities and racial injustice.

With his full name abbreviated to St. Clair Drake, he was born in 1911 in Suffolk, Virginia, not long after Dr. DuBois published his seminal work, *Souls of Black Folk.* After attending Hampton Institute and Pendle Hill, which was a Quaker graduate school outside Philadelphia, young Drake used a Rosenwald Fellowship to attend the University of Chicago in order to be trained formally in anthropology, with his doctoral degree being awarded in 1954 at the University of Chicago.

Many questioned why Drake studied anthropology, and his response was that he was initially drawn to the course because he wanted to be able to "aid in dissipating stereotypes about black people and in eliminating errors based on confusion between biological and environmental factors in accounting for observed racial differences."

After completing his doctoral dissertation fieldwork in Tiger Bay, Cardiff, Drake taught in predominantly black and white colleges and universities. However, after meeting Ghana's late president Kwame Nkrumah and Nigeria's first indigenous President Nnamdi Azikiwe, Drake's political and intellectual interests were modified, as he embraced Pan-Africanism, and the potential of assisting the emergent independent African nations. That was why he moved to West Africa, where he initially taught at the University of Liberia, when the octogenarian President W.V.S. Tubman ruled the country. Not very long after that, he received a personal invitation from Ghana to teach at University of Ghana, where he did high-quality ethnographical research until 1966, when he left Ghana as Dean of the Faculty of Social Sciences at the local University of Ghana.

Between 1946 and 1968, Professor Drake, with the support of several close intellectuals, developed and ran one of the first African studies programs in the USA, this time at Roosevelt College in Chicago. It was in 1969, after distinguishing himself in Ghana, that Drake accepted a position at Stanford University as the Head of Black Studies program. Drake remained at Stanford until his retirement in 1976, when he received the rank of Professor Emeritus. He died in 1990. As part of Drake's defined duties at Stanford University, which was very late in his long teaching career, he trained several graduate students in his beloved subject, anthropology. Agreeing that a true scholar seeks and embraces collaboration, he worked very closely with Faye Harrison of the University of Florida as well as Willie Baber also of that university. In addition, he worked with Edmund "Ted" Gordon of the University of Texas in Austin and Glen Jordan (University of Glamorgan, Wales UK). Before that he influenced the lives and studies of many undergraduate students and Roosevelt University, including the late Vera Green of Rutgers University.

Professor Drake's collaborator Faye Harrison attested to the fact that Dr. Drake's commitment to activism and scholarship—in the context of anthropology as a vehicle for change as seen in his long professional output—has been exhibited throughout his career. Furthermore, his applied research in West Africa was seen in leadership terms, but his vast activist scholarship did create an important model for many younger scholars in the humanities and social sciences, which he led in Ghana. His noted and distinguished contributions to the study of Africa in the diaspora did encourage many students, as budding scholars, to situate their obviously localized intellectual concerns as well as professional worries within a broader context of international relations, economics, and power. Dr. Drake's life and work should inspire younger scholars to help in transforming the discipline of anthropology.

Established since his death is the St. Clair Drake Fellowship, which honors his legacy, as it encourages very promising graduate students to do ethnography in North America and to present their research at professional meetings locally and internationally. Another lasting tribute is the 22nd annual St. Clair Drake Research Symposium at UC-Berkeley and at Stanford University.

CONCLUSION

Although the bulk of this study has a lot to do with St. Clair Drake, it is important to underscore further that he played a major role in making sure that several African American leaders, including Dr. King, Dr. W.E.B. DuBois, A. Philip Randolph, and others would visit Ghana. It is, indeed, remarkable that Professor Drake is being celebrated at the 22nd Annual Symposium at the University of California at Berkeley, which bears his name. The theme for the event speaks volumes for Professor Drake, who immortalized his name with his numerous accomplishments, including his contribution of useful services on the African continent as well as the various important books he authored (or co-authored) as a pioneer in Black Studies. He was the first permanent director of Stanford University's African and Afro-American Studies Program as well as a professor emeritus of sociology and anthropology at that institution.

Among his published works was *Black Metropolis: A Study of Negro Life in a Northern City* (an acclaimed 1945 book that he co-authored with Horace R. Clayton). The 830- page book, published by Harcourt and Brace, studied segregation, poverty, and discrimination in Chicago's South Side ghetto of Bronzeville. The publication has also been hailed by reviewers and fellow scholars as a landmark of objective research and one of the best urban studies produced by American scholarship. It is, therefore, not surprising that the Berkeley Symposium is named in honor of Professor Drake.

Most certainly, Professor Drake endeavored to bring fellow black leaders (or American Africans) like King, Malcolm X, DuBois, and others to Ghana when he lived and worked there; he made sure that they had a forum on University of Ghana campus to address the students, most of whom are today's leaders of Ghana. Consequently, Dr. Drake has nationally and internationally been honored for his laudable endeavors. Indeed, Professor Faye V. Harrison said it best when, inter alia, she wrote that beyond efforts to organize conferences, symposia, and producing publications on Drake's work, they also found a way to celebrate his scholarship "by nominating him for prestigious honors and awards... George Clement Bond and James Gibbs, Jr. played an important role in this endeavor, resulting in Drake's receiving fellow status in the Royal Anthropological Institute of Great Britain and Ireland (1985), a professional Achievement citation from university of Chicago Alumni Association (1987), the Society for Applied Anthropology's Bronisalw Malinowski Award (1990), honorary doctorates, and many other awards."

It is, inter alia, also confirmed that Dr. Drake's extensive Pan-Africanist connections: "His relationship with Kwame Nkrumah and the Trinidadian Pan-Africanists George Padmore and C.L. R. James while in Britain and later in Ghana during its postcolonial transition) figured prominently in his mesmerizing tales of antiracist and anticolonial politics and the accompanying quest for a form of knowledge that convincingly explains and effectively empowers."

Above all, it has been authoritatively pointed out, among other details: "St. Clair Drake's black internationalist pedagogy and scholarship were awe-inspiring. They continue to set the standard for what I understand to be the role of black intellectuals, especially those of us who claim citizenship in the world. More of us interested in transnational blackness, Pan-Africanism, and the global African Diaspora should revisit his [Drake's] work." Our own admiration and respect for the sagacious and, truly, Pan-African intellectual, who was born John Gibbs St. Clair Drake (now shortened as St. Clair Drake), prompts us to second these thoughts and stand in salute to Professor Drake with whom we had the privilege of interacting at Stanford University between the late 1980s and early 1990s! Even then, he was mellowing with age and radicalism, but he was certainly still a force to reckon with!

REFERENCES

BOOKS

Abernathy, Ralph David. 1989. And the Walls Came Tumbling Down: An Autobiography. New York: Harper & Row.

Alexander, E. Curtis. 1989. Elijah Muhammad on African-American Education. New York: ECA Associates.

Alex-Assensoh, Yvette M. 1998. *Neighborhoods, Family, and Political Behavior in Urban America.* New York. Garland Publishing, Inc, and The Maxine Goodman Levin center (Cleveland State University).

Andoh, Samuel K.. 2014. *Essentials of Money, Banking and Financial Institutions (Developing World).* Lanham, Maryland: Lexington Books.

Assensoh, A.B. 1984. *Rev. Dr. Martin Luther King, Jr. and America's Quest for Racial Integration.* Ilfracombe, Devon, UK: Arthur H. Stockwell Limited (Book Publishers).

———. 1998. *African Political Leadership: Jomo Kenyatta, Kwame Nkrumah and Julius K. Nyerere.* Malabar, Florida: Krieger Publishers.

Assensoh, A.B., and Yvette M. Alex-Assensoh. 2001. *African Military History and Politics, 1900-Present.* New York: Palgrave-Macmillan of St. Martin's Press.

———. 2014. *Malcolm X; A Biography.* Santa Barbara, California: Greenwood Press.

Azikiwe, Nnamdi. 1970. My Odyssey: An Autobiography. Westport, CT.: Praeger.

Ball, Jared A., and Todd Burroughs. 2012. *A Lie of Reinvention: Correcting Manning Marable's Malcolm X.* Baltimore, MD: Black Classic Press.

Boyd, Herb, Ron Daniels, Karenga, and Haki R. Madhubuti. 2012. *By any means necessary: Malcolm X-- Real, Not Reinvented : Critical Conver-*

sations on Manning Marable's Biography of Malcolm X. Chicago, IL: Third World Press.

Branch, Taylor. 1998. *Pillar of Fire: America in the King Years, 1963-1965.*New York: Simon and Schuster.

Breitman, George, ed. *1990. Malcolm X Speaks: Selected Speeches and Statements.* New York: Grove, Weidenfield Publisher.

_____ 1967. *The Last Year of Malcolm X: The Evolution of a Revolutionary.* New York: Pathfinder Press.

_____, ed. 1970. *By Any Means Necessary: Speeches, Interviews, and a Letter by Malcolm X.* New York: Pathfinder Press.

_____, Herman Porter, and Baxter Smith. 1976. *The Assassination of Malcolm X.* New York: Pathfinder Press.

Carson, Clayborne, ed. 1998. *The Autobiography of Martin Luther King, Jr. New* York: Warren Books/.

_____, ed. 1991. *Malcolm X: The FBI File.* New York: Carroll & Graf Publishers.

Cashman, Sean D. 1991. *African-Americans and the Quest for Civil rights, 1900-1990.* New York: New York University Press.

Clark, Steve, ed. 1991. *Malcolm X Talks to Young People: Speeches in the United States, Britain, and Africa.* New York: Pathfinder Press..

_____, ed.1992. *February 1965: The Final Speeches.* New York: Pathfinder Press.

Clarke, John Henrik. 1990. *Malcolm X: The Man and His Times.* Trenton, NJ: Africa World Press.

Clegg, Claude Andrew. 1997. *An Original man: The Life and Times of Elijah Muhammad .* New York: St. Martin's Press.

———. 2004. *The Price of Liberty: African Americans and the Making of Liberia.* Chapel Hill: University of North Carolina Press.

———. 2010. *Troubled Ground: A Tale of Murder, Lynching, and reckoning in the New South.* Urbana, Chicago, and Springfield, Illinois: University of Illinois Press.

DeCaro, Louis A. 1996. *On the side of my people: a religious life of Malcolm X.* New York: New York University Press.

DuBois, W.E.B. 1903. (1909). *The Souls of Black Folk.* Chicago, Illinois: A.C. McClure & Co.

Dyson, Michael E. 1995. *Making Malcolm: The Myth and Meaning of Malcolm X.* New York: Oxford University Press.

El-Amin, Mustafa. 1991. *The Religion of Islam and the Nation of Islam: What Is the Difference?* Newark, NJ: El-Amin Productions.

Epps, Archie, ed. *The Speeches of Malcolm X at Harvard.* New York: Morrow.

Esedebe, P. Olisanwuche. 1982. *Pan-Africanism: The Idea and Movement, 1776–1963.* Washington, DC: Howard University Press.

Essien-Udom, E.U. *Black Nationalism: A Search for an Identity in America.* Chicago: University of Chicago Press.

Gaines, Kevin K. 2006. *American Africans in Ghana.* Chapel Hill, NC: University of North Carolina Press.

Gallen, David, ed.1992. *Malcolm As They Knew Him.* New York: Carroll and Graf.

Garrow, David J. 1986. *Bearing the Cross: Martin Luther king, Jr., and the Southern Christian Leadership Conference.* New York: Vintage Books.

Garvey, Marcus. 1968. *Philosophy and Opinions of Marcus Garvey.* Edited by Amy Jacques Garvey. New York: Arno Press.

Garvey, Amy Jacques, and Marcus Garvey. 1977. *More philosophy and opinions of Marcus Garvey.* London: Cass.

Garvey, Marcus. 1987. *Marcus Garvey: Life and Lessons.* Edited by Robert A Hill and Barbara Bair. Berkeley: University of California Press.

Goldman, Peter. 1971. *The Life and Death of Malcolm X.* Urbana, Illinois: University of Illinois Press, 1971, Urbana, Illinois.

Haley, Alex. 1974. *Roots New York:* Vanguard Press.

Hedgeman, Anna A. 1964. *The Trumpet Sounds: A Memoir of Negro Leadership.* New York: Holt, Rinehart and Winston.

Jenkins, Robert L., and Mfanya D. Tryman. 2002. *The Malcolm X Ency-clopedia.* Westport, CT.: Greenwood Publishing Company.

Johnson, Charles, and John McCluskey. 1997. *Black Men Speaking.* Bloomington: Indiana University Press.

Karim, Benjamin, ed. 1971. *The End of White World Supremacy: Four Speeches by Malcolm X.* New York: Monthly Review Press. Press, Boston, MA.

Kelley, Robin D.G. 1994. *Race Rebels. New York:* Free Press.

———. 2003. *Freedom Dreams: The Black Radical Imagination.* Boston, MA: Beacon Press.

King, Coretta Scott. 1969. *My Life With Martin Luther King, Jr.* New York: Holt, Rinehart and Winston.

Kravchnko, Svitlana, and John E. Bonine, 2008. *Human Rights and the Environment.* Durham, NC: Carolina Academic Press.

Lacy, Leslie Alexander. 1970. *The Rise and Fall of a Proper Negro; An Au-tobiography.* [New York]: Macmillan.

Lomax, Louis E. 1962. *The Negro Revolt* New York: Harper & Row.

———. 1987. *To Kill a Black Man.* Reprint. Los Angeles, CA: Halloway House.

Malcolm X, with Alex Haley. 1999. *The Autobiography of Malcolm X.* New York: Ballantine Books.

———. 1965. *Two Speeches by Malcolm X.* New York: Pathfinder Press.

———. 1967. *Malcolm X on Afro-American History.* New York: Merit Pub-lishers.

Marable, Manning. 2011. *Malcolm X: A Life of Reinvention.* New York: Viking.

Moxon, James. 1984. *Volta: Man's Greatest Lake: The Story of Ghana's Akosombo Dam.* London, UK: Andre Deutsch Limited (Publishers).

Nkrumah, Kwame. 1957. *Ghana: The Autobiography of Kwame Nkrumah.* London: Thomas Nelson and Sons.

Perry, Bruce, ed. 1989. *The Last Speeches of Malcolm X.* New York: Pathfinder Press.

_____. *Malcolm: The Life of a Man Who Changed Black America.* Barrytown, NY: Station Hill Press.

Provenzo, Eugene, and F. Edmund Abaka, eds. 2012. *DuBois on Africa.* Walnut Creek, California: Left Coast Press.

Quaison-Sackey, Alex. 1963. *Africa Unbound: Reflections of an African Statesman.* New York: Praeger.

Reddick, Lawrence D. 1959. *Crusader without Violence: Biography of Martin Luther King, Jr.* New York: Harper & Row.

Robeson, Paul. 1993. *Paul Robeson, Jr. Speaks To America.* New Brunswick, NJ: Rutgers University Press.

Robinson, Randall. 1998. *Defending The Spirit: A Black Life In America.* New York: The Penguin Group/Putnam.

Sayles, William. 1994. *From Civil Rights to Black Liberation: Malcolm X and the Organization of Organization of Afro-American Unity.* Boston, MA: South End Publishers.

Sherwood, Marika. 2011. *Malcolm X visits abroad: April 1964 - February 1965.* Hollywood, CA: Tsehai Publishers.

PERIODICALS/PAMPHLETS

Adem, Seifudein. 2015. "A Tribute to Ali Mazrui". *Transition Magazine* 117, (July/August): 195–197).

Allen, Jr. Ernest. 1994. "Satokata Takahashi and the Flowering of Black Nationalism." *Black Scholar Journal* 24, no.1: 23–46.

Ansari, Z.I. 1981. "Aspects of Black Muslim Theology." *Studia Islamica Journal* 53: 137 –76.

_____. 1985. "W.D. Muhammad: The Making of a Black Muslim leader, 1933-1961." *American Journal of Islamic Social Sciences* 22: 245–62.

Barboza, Steven. 1992. "Muslims: A Divided Legacy." *Emerge Magazine* April: 26–32.

Battle, V. DuWayne. 1988. "The Influence of Al-Islam in America on the Black Community." *Black Scholar* 19: 33–41.

Brown, Warren, and J. M. Stephens, Jr. 1972. "Police Probe Killings in Baton Rouge." *Jet Magazine* January: 6–9.

Editor. 1979. "Commentary: Elijah Muhammad's 13 Illegitimate Children Must Share Estate: Court." *Jet Magazine* 25: 8–9.

Haley, Alex. 1969. "Mr. Muhammad Speaks." *Readers Digest* March: 100–104.

Hatchett, John F. 1962. "The Moslem [Muslim] Influences among American Negroes." *Journal of Human Relations* 10, no. 4: 375–82.

Jones, Jr., Oliver. 1983. "The Black Muslim Movement and the American Constitutional System." *Journal of Black Studies* 13, no. 4: 417–37.

Khalifa H. K. 1988. *The Legacy of the Honorable Elijah Muhammad* (pamphlet). Newport News, Va.: United Brothers Communications Systems.

Koster, Mickie M. 2015. "Malcolm X, The Mau Mau, And Kenya's New Revolutionaries: A Legacy of Transnationalism." *Journal of African-American History* 100, No. 2 (Winter): 250–272).

Lightfoot, Claude. 1962. "Negro Nationalism and the Black Muslims." *Political Affairs Journal* 41, no. 7: 3–20.

Lincoln, C. Eric. 1965. "The Meaning of Malcolm X." *Christian Century Magazine* 7 (April): 431–33.

Massaquoi, Hans. 1964. "Mystery of Malcolm X." *Ebony Magazine* (December): 38–48.

Parks, Gordon. 1965. "The violent End of the Man Called Malcolm X." *Life Magazine*, March 5: 26–31.

Russel, Carlos E. 1964. "Exclusive Interview with Malcolm X." *Liberator Magazine.* (May): 12–13).

Shabazz, Betty. 1969. "The Legacy of My Husband, Malcolm X." *Ebony Magazine.* (June): 172–74.

Smith Christopher E. 1993."Black Muslims and the Development of Prisoners' Rights." *Journal of Black Studies* 24, no. 2: 131–46.

Tyler, L. L. 1996. "The Protestant Ethic among the Black Muslims." *Phylon* 27, no. 1: 5–14.

White, Abbie. 1964. "Christian Elements in negro American Muslim Religious Beliefs". *Phylon* 25, no.4: 382–88.

Woodford, John. 1991. "Testing America's Promise of Free Speech: Muhammad Speaks in the 1960s." *Voices of the African Diaspora Magazine* 7, no.3: 3–16.

Wiley, Charles W. 1965. "Who Was Malcolm X?" *National Review,* March 13: 239–240.

AUDIO SOURCES

1959. On "Minister Malcolm X and Minister Wallace D. Muhammad"(85 minutes).

1960. "A Weekly radio broadcast: Mr. Muhammad Speaks" (51 minutes) Malcolm X speaks on The Work and Mission of the Hon Elijah Muhammad.

May 1, 1962. "The Crisis of Racism": Malcolm X, James Farmer, William Worthy (15 minutes).

December, 1962. Malcolm X on "The Black Man's History" (87 minutes).

June, 1963. Malcolm X speaks on "The Black Revolution" at the invitation of Adam Clayton Powell, Abyssinian Baptist Church, New York City. (26 minutes).

August 10, 1963. "Harlem Unity Rally" (116 minutes).

January 23, 1963. Malcolm X speaks on "The Race Problem in America" at the invitation of the African Students Association and the campus chapter of the NAACP, Michigan State University, East Lansing, MI. (54 minutes).

November 10, 1963. Malcolm X delivers a speech, titled "Message to the Grass Roots" (46 minutes) Northern Grass Roots Leadership Conference Detroit, Michigan.

December 13, 1964. "OAAU Rally, Audubon Ballroom, New York City" (70 minutes) Malcolm X on the Afro-American problem as a world problem, with Dick Gregory and Babu.

December 16, 1964. Malcolm at "Harvard Law School Forum" (50 minutes). Malcolm X on the African Revolution and Its Impact on the American Negro.

December 31, 1964. Malcolm X delivers "Speech to Mississippi Youth, New York City (15 minutes). Malcolm tells a group of young people "think for yourself"

1964. Malcolm X's "Press Conference in New York City" (7 minutes) Malcolm X calls press conference to clarify position in the struggle, regarding politics and non-violence.

INTERNET SOURCES

Carson, Clayborne. Editor. Autobiography of Martin Luther King, Jr. (among credible quotable sources, where Malcolm X and other black leaders are mentioned or discussed). http://www.stanford.edu/group/King/publications,autobiography/chp_21.htm.

Pastors & Ministers. "Eulogy for the Young Victims of the Sixteenth Street Baptist Church Bombing" delivered at Sixth Avenue Baptist Church in Birmingham, Alabama. http://www..stanford.edu/group/King/speeches/pub/Eulogy_for_the_martyred_children.html.

Formwalt, Lee W. "Moving Forward by recalling the Past...". http://members.surfsouth.com/~mtzion/movementshistory.htm.

Gittinger, Ted, and Allen Fisher. "Lyndon B. Johnson Champions the Civil Rights Act of 1964." http://www.archives.gov/publications/prologue/2004/summer/civil-rights-act-1.html.

President John F. Kennedy's "June 11, 1963 speech to American people". http://www.jfklibrary.org/j061163.htm.

President Lyndon B. Johnson's "American Promise Speech of March 15, 1965 to American People. http://www.lbjlib.utexas.edu/johnson/ archives.hom/speeches.hom/650315.asp.

Ture, Kwame (Stokely Carmichael). "Speech on Black Power and the Black People of America." http://www.americanrhetoric.com/speeches/ stokelycarmichaelblackpower.html.

MANUSCRIPT COLLECTIONS

Alex Haley Papers at Schomburg Center for Research in Black Culture. The New York Public Library.

Boston University Library's Special Collection (Martin Luther King, Jr., Papers).

C. Eric Lincoln Papers. Special Collections of Clark Atlanta University.

Du Bois Centre and Archives, Accra, Ghana, West Africa.

Ghana National Archives, Accra, Ghana, West Africa (Kwame Nkrumah/ Malcolm X/Graham DuBois' Correspondence).

Mooreland-Spingarn Research Center of Howard University.

Northeastern University Special Collections, Boston, MA.

Beinecke Rare Book Library, Yale University, New Haven.

Morehouse College Special King Collections (Official Acquisition), Atlanta, Georgia. The Malcolm X Project & Oral History Project at Columbia University, New York.

The Papers of Malcolm X at Schomburg Center for Research in Black Culture of New York Public Library, Harlem, New York.

CENTERS FOR RESEARCH

The Schomburg Center for Research in Black Culture of New York Public Library, Harlem, New York.

Ghana National Archives, Accra, Ghana, West Africa.

DuBois Centre and Archives, Accra, Ghana, West Africa.

Mooreland-Spingarn Research Center of Howard University.

Northeastern University Special Collections, Boston, MA.

Beinecke Rare Book Library, Yale University, New Haven, CT.

Boston University Library's Special Collection (Martin Luther King, Jr. Papers). Morehouse College Special King Collections (Official Acquisition), Atlanta, Georgia.

The Malcolm X Project & Oral History Project at Columbia University, New York.

About the Authors

A.B. ASSENSOH

A.B. Assensoh is professor emeritus of Indiana University and Courtesy Professor Emeritus and Mentor for international students at University of Oregon in Eugene, Oregon, USA. Author and co-author of numerous books, Professor Assensoh earned his MA and PhD degrees in history from New York University (NYU) as well as his graduate law (LLM) degree from the School of Law of University of Oregon. He has held several postdoctoral fellowships at various universities, including Harvard University, Oxford, Virginia, Emory, and also a Fulbright-Hays Faculty Fellowship for research in Southeast Asia.

YVETTE M. ALEX-ASSENSOH

Yvette M. Alex-Assensoh is professor of political science and Vice-President of Equity and Inclusion at University of Oregon. A former dean for the Office of Women's Affairs (OWA) and professor of political science on the flagship Bloomington campus of Indiana University, Professor Alex-Assensoh is author and co-author of several books as well as refereed and popular articles. In 1999–2000, she served as a Fulbright Scholar at University of Zagreb in Croatia. She has received several grants and other fellowships, including serving as ACE Fellow. She and A.B. Assensoh are parents of two sons, Kwadwo and Livingston.

Index

Quaison-Sackey, Alex (*continued*), 32–33, 52, 109–112

Qur'an, 35

racial discrimination, 20, 34, 78

racism, xii, xxvi, 10, 13, 32, 56–57, 61, 74, 77–79, 92, 100, 106, 111

Rastafarian, 42

Rawlings, John, 111

Reith Lecture Series, 78

Republic of Biafra, xi

Republic of Liberia, 75

Riverside Church, 90

Robinson, Jackie, 21

Robinson, Randall, 64–65

Rupert, Maurice, 17

Rusk, Dean, 71

Sanders, Betty, xiv, xviii, xxi, xxvii, 10, 19–20, 22, 24, 36, 48, 85, 106–107, 109–110, 112

Saudi Arabia, 23, 34, 37, 43

Savimbi, Jonas, 56, 58–65

Schomburg Center for Research in Black Culture, 111

Second World War, 2, 7

Selassie, Haile, 42, 77

Senegal, 23, 31, 49

Seseko, Mobutu, 59

Shabazz, Atallah, 6

Shabazz, Betty, xiv, xviii, xxi, xxvii, 10, 19–20, 22, 24, 36, 48, 85, 106–107, 109–110, 112

Shabazz, Gamilah Lumumba, xiv, xxi

Shabazz, Ilyasah, xiv, 20

Shabazz, Malika, xiv

Shabazz, Quibilah, xiv, 22

Sharpton, Al, 11

Sheik Abeid Amani Karume, Sheik Abeid Amani, 69, 82

Slovo, Joe, xxii

South Africa, xviii, xxi–xxii, 5, 57, 64, 100

South African Development Community (SADC), 9

South African Truth Commission, xxii

Southern Christian Leadership Conference (SCLC), 3, 90–92

Southern Rhodesia, 72

Steve Biko,Steve, xxii, 64

Student Nonviolent Coordinating Committee (SNCC), 21, 91

Sub-Sahara Africa, 41

Sudan, 20, 41–42

Suez Canal, 29

Sukarno, 29

Tanganyika, 68–69, 82

Tanzania, 7, 24, 52, 68–74, 81–83, 100–101, 108–109

Tarzarfa Railways, 82

Telli, Boubacar Diallo, 7, 9, 30–31, 33–34, 52, 77–80, 110

Thatcher, Margaret, 65

Time to Break the Silence (speech), 90

Toure, Sekou, 9, 31, 38, 52, 79, 101

traditional beliefs, 42

traitor, 113

TransAfrica, 64–65

Tubman, William V.S., 75–76, 139

Ture, Kwame, xxiv, 91

Turkey, 41

Uganda, 24, 72, 101

Uganda, 24, 72, 101

Umrah, 40

UN General Assembly, 7

Union of the Peoples Northern Angola, 59

CPSIA information can be obtained at www.ICGtesting.com
Printed in the USA
BVOW08*1731010416

R6888000001B/R68880PG441514BVX1B/1/P